YOU'VE GOT THIS

BEC BROWN

Bec has been working as a professional communicator for twenty years, beginning as a vocalist and vocal coach, then retraining to become a PR professional.

She's the founder and Managing Director of The Comms Department, a PR, corporate communications and crisis management agency, where she and her team work with some of Australia's biggest and best-known media, entertainment, travel and lifestyle brands.

At the 2019 Mumbrella CommsCon Awards, Australia and New Zealand's most prestigious PR industry awards, Bec was one of five finalists for PR Professional of the Year. Every year The Comms Department has entered the awards it has been shortlisted for Small PR Agency of the Year.

Bec's professional experience is also backed by study – a Graduate Diploma in Media and Communications, Certificates in Social Psychology and Negotiation, and a Bachelor of Music.

INGA CAMPBELL

Inga is an illustrator, designer and the founder of Inkling Design, a design studio that offers art direction, branding and custom illustration.

Since studying a Bachelor of Design with a major in Graphic Design, Inga has worked as a professional designer for seventeen years, first at *Girlfriend* magazine before moving on to roles such as Deputy Art Director at *Cosmopolitan* and Art Director at *GRAZIA*. Inga now works with clients all over the globe, and her illustrations appear in some of the world's best-known magazines, as prized artworks, on garments, as large-scale murals and, now, in a book.

Inga, Mike and their daughter Andy recently packed, donated or sold everything they had in Australia and went on a year-long adventure through North America, with Inga successfully running Inkling Design while they travelled and explored.

YOU'VE GOT THIS

The essential career handbook for creative women

Bec Brown

illustrations by Inga Campbell

CONTENTS

We're going to cover:

WELL HEY

do any of these questions apply to you?

- Are you a creative person?
- Do you ever feel worried or anxious about your career?
- Do you want to enjoy your career so that it remains a passion rather than something that sucks the life out of you?
- Do you work or want to work in a creative industry such as PR, marketing, media, entertainment, photography or design?
- Have you thought about starting your own business?
- Do you want to learn some secrets that will equip you to face the challenges of today's professional environment head-on?
- Would you like to feel confident that you're living up to your true potential in your work?

If you answered YES to any of these questions, then this book is for YOU.

As two creative professionals with over forty years of experience combined, both in corporate environments and in creating our own thriving businesses, we're going to give you all the shortcuts and tips we wish someone had given us back when we were starting out. These tips will make you happier in your work and increase both your earning potential and opportunities for promotion.

We know that managing your career can be tricky, but we also know that you've got this. And by the time you've finished this book, you'll know it too.

> Before we start – go grab a notebook.
>
> On page one, write:
>
> YOU'VE GOT THIS.
>
> As you make your way through this book, you can write down notes and record your responses to the exercises we've set. We promise that this act of writing down your thoughts will not only help to clarify things for you, it will also help motivate you to action. So let's get started.

AUTHOR'S NOTE

(though it's actually all about YOU)

My name's Bec, and these next few pages tell my story.

I'll also introduce you to Inga.

But before I go on . . . WHY should you hear our stories first?

I'll reveal this in a few pages and it'll all make sense.

But – spoiler alert – these pages are actually all about YOU.

So, read on . . .

I'm constantly approached for advice – by graduates wanting to intern with me, those who are thinking of starting a business, creatives who don't like working in 'corporate' jobs and want to take a different approach, and others who don't really understand how PR works but want to. The media and our clients have frequently told me, 'We wish other PRs worked in the way that you and your team do.' And it's true: we do work differently to many others in our industry. This book reveals some of the secrets to that.

Inga and I both just turned forty and see the small, silly mistakes that many capable young professionals make today – mistakes we both made when we were in the early stages of our careers too.

We wish that a trusted mentor had simply handed us this book and said, 'Read this, and then ask me if you have any questions.'

Would we have taken ALL of it on board?

Probably not. We would still have needed to explore and make our own mistakes and learn from them.

But a shortcut would have definitely helped a lot.

So who am I to be dishing out advice?

Well, I own and run a PR and comms agency.

A damn successful one, TBH.

But I didn't set out to.

I started out as a musician – mostly singing. I sang pop, jazz, musical theatre and opera. I've appeared on screen and radio, on stage with bands and in shows, have been a singing teacher in primary and high schools and have even been a children's entertainer.

Then I pivoted.

I retrained and began a career in public relations, working on campaigns spanning entertainment, media, travel, food, fitness, retail, medicine, finance and more.

These days, as well as running the business side of my agency, I work as its Communications Director. This means I create public relations strategies, work with journalists, write, edit, create content for social media and, more often than anyone probably realises thanks to the level of confidentiality, manage crisis communications.

One thing that's common to both music and PR is communication: telling stories with a purpose, assessing how they're being received, and continuing – and sometimes changing – the conversation that everyone's having.

It's powerful and I seriously love it.

Which is why I've been doing it for twenty years.

Today I'm going to let you in on a few secrets. Here's secret #1.

> I had a really weird way of arriving at where I am today.
>
> I feel like you should know this because, chances are, your career journey won't be a straight line either. And if it's a squiggly mess that jumps from place to place, you need to know that's okay.

I grew up on a farm near a tiny country town in South Australia. There were forty kids in my primary school, and less than 200 in my high school.

I was a good singer and decided that was what I wanted to be when I grew up. I dreamed of being in musicals on NYC's Broadway or London's West End.

I felt lucky that I had a sense of direction because many of my school friends didn't. But I also wished that I'd chosen something with a more direct path. If I wanted to be a doctor or lawyer, the path would be straightforward (though far from easy). But the path to becoming a singer? Much less clear-cut. It'd not only require learning to be really great at singing, but also knowing how to dance and act, looking a certain way for a role, sometimes being a certain size, getting to know the right people, and being in the right place at the right time, for the right role, with the right show.

My family weren't in show business – dad was a hospital nurse and pastor and mum worked two jobs as an admin executive. But they always supported their four kids in their unique pursuits. That meant driving me, the youngest, fifty kilometres to singing and dancing lessons and encouraging me to practise. They were also big on education and having something to fall back on. So if I wanted to be a singer, they said, I should get a music degree so I had the option of becoming a music teacher if the performing thing didn't work out.

But my little country high school didn't offer music as a subject. And my parents didn't have the money to send me to an expensive private school in the city. There was a really respected public school that specialised in music, but it was a three-hour drive away in the big smoke of Adelaide. After begging my parents to see if we could find a way for me to go there, they said I could audition and sit the test and, if I got in, they'd look for a way to make the finances work for years 11 and 12.

I applied, got an audition date, then practised and cram-studied. My audition and test went well, so all I could do was wait.

This was 1994. Email didn't hit the mainstream in Australia for a couple more years, so I had to wait for a letter to arrive at our little town's post office to tell me my fate.

My parents wanted to open it first. I looked at them reading it, feeling sick. 'Well, it looks like you're moving to Adelaide,' Dad said.

Full disclosure: I was only a slightly above-average student, and a bit lazy in that I only did well in the subjects that interested me (music, English, art, PE) and sucked at those that didn't (maths and science). I was also now going to be living away from home, boarding with family friends and attempting 'adulting' for the first time. Safe to say, I frequently failed at it – as for many sixteen-year-olds, managing a budget, cooking nutritious meals and keeping up with my washing weren't high on my list of priorities.

But after graduating high school, I auditioned to get into Adelaide University's Conservatorium of Music. Thankfully the audition was worth more than my predictably only slightly above-average year 12 grades and I got in and, while earning a Bachelor of Music, started performing professionally straight away.

And for seven years, across seven cities in five countries, I performed my little heart out.

But, as you know, I'm no longer in music. So what changed?

At twenty-five I had a quarter-life crisis and realised that I wasn't very happy.

As much as I loved performing, it was an incredibly difficult life. Moving around so much meant being away from close friends and family, and this was back when the world wasn't as connected, when we didn't have smartphones or social media. Most of the time I worked at night, and going to work when most people are coming home to see their loved ones can be really isolating. And as a morning person who loves sunshine and being outdoors, this was extra tricky. Added to this was the pressure of being under the microscope – judged daily on my looks, weight, sound and physical ability, I battled an eating disorder, anxiety and depression.

If I was starting my performing career now, it would be a lot easier. There's so much more support around today – we're better connected online, there's more structure, performers are better cared for, and there's more diversity in roles. Not to mention how easy it is now to reach and develop your audience thanks to YouTube and social media. But timing can be everything, and in the late 90s and early 2000s, you either had to suck it up or move on.

On top of that, I knew deep down that while I was a good singer and an adequate dancer, I wasn't brilliant. Even with excellent training, it was going to take next-level practice and persistence to be a star. Because I didn't want to just be in the chorus, I wanted to play the lead. And frankly, without that practice and persistence, I wasn't good enough. My heart clearly wasn't in it, otherwise I would have found a way.

So it was time to let performing go. I'd also just had my heart broken by a boy, which made me crave a change of scene even more.

Spurred on by this timely catalyst, I started thinking about what else I enjoyed and was good at. I'd always liked writing and storytelling and was a total grammar nerd. I was also naturally curious and investigative, always asking people 'why?' I considered journalism, but then thought that this thing called public relations might be a good fit. Confession time: I didn't really understand what PR was. All I knew was that you needed to love the news and understand how the media worked, and that you could work with journalists and producers to promote things. And because I loved magazines, television and radio, and was promoting myself for stage roles and for my band,

I thought I'd like it. (I had little idea then of what a great public relations professional can do, and the power and influence you can have to create exciting change.)

So after moving to Sydney, where I didn't know a single person, while working as a temp executive assistant during the day and singing at night to pay my rent and bills, I went back to uni and did a Graduate Diploma in Media and Communications online, majoring in PR.

And although I freaked out a little about leaving the music industry and having to let go of my long-held dream, I slowly fell in love with PR (and, a couple of years later, with someone else, who later became my husband).

Towards the end of my studies, I landed my first official comms gig as a PR executive at a small agency. Aside from my education and the presentation skills I'd developed as a performer, what helped me get the job was the corporate experience I'd gained working as an assistant to a CEO (which is proof that all experience can help you land a job in your dream industry, even if it's not 100 per cent related).

However, I CRIED MY EYES OUT most mornings on the bus to work.

It was all so new and difficult.

I was doing PR work for industries I wasn't very interested in.

I felt totally out of my depth.

And I was starting at the bottom, earning way less than I had been performing.

But I kept going because I knew I needed a change. And boy was I learning. The job was particularly tough because I had a boss with the highest of standards, which meant I was under close, often harsh, scrutiny every day. But as hard as it was, I developed quickly because of it.

And it paid off.

One of my most exciting jobs came soon afterwards – I spent five years as Senior PR Manager for the largest record company in the world, Universal Music, working with some of the best-known artists and celebrities of our time. The job involved working across twenty artists at once, dealing directly with their managers, media and sponsors, being up at 4 am for breakfast TV and radio, going to bed at 1 am after gigs, constantly travelling, and coping with time differences between Australia, the US, the UK and Europe.

But I was earning excellent money with great bonuses, staying in five-star hotels, and had the chance to do both creative and commercial work every single day.

It was fast, furious, fabulous, exciting and exhausting all at once.

I learnt how to be a great publicist – to know exactly what journalists wanted, when they needed it, and how they liked to be communicated with. I discovered what each stakeholder in the business and industry wanted and why it was best to adapt to suit each of them. And I realised the value of good team management and the best way to organise my time.

While I didn't want to leave an incredible company full of bright, brilliant people, or lose the amazing perks of my job, at thirty-two I still yearned to run my own show and only work on projects I was completely passionate about. And, as I'd discovered when I broadened my world view, I enjoyed many things outside of music.

So eight years ago I set up my own PR company, The Comms Department.

We're a small team – there are five of us across three cities – but we work with some of the biggest and most successful brands in the country.

And I've also intentionally set up the business so that instead of having to make a drudging commute to and from an office every day, we all work from home, on the road, or from our clients' offices.

It's the best way to service media in a 24/7 world, but it also allows me and my team to work to our strengths. I'm a massive morning person so I start as early as I want. We can all take a gym/dance/swim/yoga break whenever we want to, and we don't waste time stuck in traffic morning and night.

Other team members who have kids can get them off to child care, or be at home when they get home from school. Being able to do our job anywhere also means we have the ability to travel the world.

And I'm earning more now than I would be if I'd stayed working as a performer or for someone else.

Sounds good, huh?

So here's secret #2.

> There was no grand plan.
>
> None.

Setting up The Comms Department was initially a huge accident.

And most of the time, it was absolutely terrifying.

Sure, there were some strategic goals along the way, especially after year three, but when I started the business, I didn't ultimately set out to create the company we have today.

It all grew and evolved naturally.

And when I look back, I can see that each step came when I was ready to handle it (even if it didn't feel that way at the time).

> **And only after assessing whether each stage was right for me and was going to allow me to lead a happy life did I move forward with any of it.**

All of this came from two things.

A burning desire to:

1. promote people, products and ideas that I'm genuinely passionate about and believe in
2. work with brilliant people.

So what's my definition of brilliant people?

They're authentic, smart and creative.

They value me and what I do for them, just as I value them and all they do.

And above all, they're kind.

These two desires may have led me to where I am today but they've also been supported by a few things:

- hard work and long hours
- attention to detail and to important things happening around me
- being adaptable, resilient and ethical
- supportive friends, family and colleagues.

You'll notice that I didn't list money as one of my desires.

That's because I never put it ahead of my two other priorities – doing brilliant work with brilliant people.

And because of that, the money has always flowed in.

Starting with no external funding and just one client, The Comms Department has been profitable from day one, and year on year we've increased our earnings.

> **If there's a market for what you do and you're good at it, are ethical and adaptable, and place a value on yourself and your time, I believe that you will never have a problem earning a great income.**

Luck is another thing that gets a small mention.

I list it with hesitation, as it's easy to look at people who are doing well and think they've just been 'lucky'.

Maybe it depends on what your definition of 'lucky' is. While I wasn't born into great wealth and my parents don't know anything about entertainment, media or running your own business, I *was* born into a supportive family who believed in me and taught me how to be resourceful and why it's important to be of service to those around you. Unconsciously, they demonstrated that working towards purposeful and meaningful goals that are unique to you will make you happier. While cheering me on, they were also at times my greatest critics. And although that was hard, we need critics, either to make us face reality or perhaps even to spur us on more. They would also teach me by example to try and be humble and to keep my ego in check.

I then left home at sixteen and was thrown into the deep end. And because of that, I quickly learnt how to swim.

To me, that's incredible luck that I will be forever grateful for.

I also have highly successful friends who didn't come from money OR have the support of family, and they've thrived in spite of this.

> **That's because, to an extent, you make your own luck.**
>
> **I've found that the harder and smarter I work, the more open and curious I am, the more willing and ready I am to jump on opportunities when they arise, and the more grateful I am for every little thing I already have in my life, the luckier I get.**

IF THERE'S A MARKET
FOR WHAT YOU DO AND
YOU'RE GOOD AT IT,
ARE ETHICAL AND ADAPTABLE,
AND PLACE A VALUE ON
YOURSELF AND YOUR TIME,
I BELIEVE THAT YOU WILL
NEVER HAVE A PROBLEM
EARNING A *great income*

> **I've learnt a lot about success over the years, and the biggest take-home is that we each have our own definition and measure of it, which, importantly, we each get to choose.**

And that's a great thing.

But it's only great if you understand that you'll always be happier when you're meeting *your own* measure of success, not someone else's.

For example, I've discovered that I'm not driven by things; I'm driven by experiences.

Don't get me wrong, I like 'things' – beautiful clothes, shoes, handbags, homes, hotels, cars and swimming pools. Seriously, who doesn't?!

But for me, they'll never replace moments in time – being with someone you love, laughing until you cry at some terrible joke with someone who gets you, feeling the warmth of the sun on your skin, diving into the ocean on a hot day, eating a delicious meal, putting a smile on someone else's face, hugging your nieces, nephews, cats or dogs, arriving in a new country and hearing different languages, smelling unfamiliar scents and feeling like a complete alien, or just snuggling into a freshly made bed with clean sheets.

So it's time and health that I value – moments that can be enjoyed, collected and remembered with great pleasure.

> **Over time, you learn to surround yourself with people who have a similar idea of success to yours.**

That's not to say that you can't enjoy or learn from others who are different to you; but being with people who value the same things as you will make your life infinitely more enjoyable and (to drive home the point) more successful.

So why have I told you all these things?

Because it's now up to you to decide.

Is choosing your own path important to you?

Are you willing to have an open mind and try something new?

If the answer is yes, you're going to benefit from the tips and tricks in this book. And you'll get to take advantage of all the lessons that I had to learn (mostly the hard way!) so that you can create a better career and a happier, more fulfilling life.

This is also the perfect time to introduce you to the amazing Inga Campbell.

She has drawn all the beautiful illustrations in this book.

I met Inga through her husband, Mike, who was a colleague of mine at Universal Music. Other than being one of life's positive and interesting people, Mike's gone on to become the founder of www.liveimmediately.com, an online, podcast and events platform that helps people to live more with less, align their values and prioritise their time so they can do more of the things they love, with people they love.

Inga is an illustrator and designer who founded Inkling Design, a design studio that offers art direction, branding and illustration.

She's worked in design for seventeen years. Prior to starting her own business, she worked at *Girlfriend* magazine before taking on Art Director roles at *GRAZIA* and *Cosmopolitan*.

Inga has been responsible for my PR agency's branding, and has also done all the branding for my Bec Brown Brownies (a little side hustle I have), which I gift to clients, media and industry friends. (Check them out on Instagram by looking up #BecBrownBrownies.)

It's rare to find someone who can deliver such incredible, professional work and who is also an absolute joy to be around. I've watched, so impressed, as her business has bloomed and thrived.

As well as being a clever creative with a successful commercial business, Inga's also an adventurer and explorer. A few years ago, Inga, Mike and their daughter Andy decided to leave Australia and go on a year-long adventure through North America, with Inga running the business as she travelled.

Over eight years of working together, I have discovered that Inga and I share a very similar view of success; we both believe that sometimes it's the journey towards your goals that holds all the secrets.

So, throughout this book, you'll also be hearing from Inga, who will share some bite-sized pieces of wisdom gathered from her years of working in publishing and design and running her own business.

As you read, consider Inga and me your very own Creative Career Coaches.

But enough about us.

It's over to you.

YOU'VE *got* THIS

CHAPTER 1

YOUR PROFESSIONAL PERSONAL BRAND

and why it's the most important part of your career you'll ever invest in

Every day of your life, you're on show.

In person, your audience is your family, friends, colleagues, and those you come across in your day-to-day activities – at the cafe where you get your coffee, at the gym, or at the park where you walk your dog (or cat, no judgement here).

Online it's more obvious – your audience is your social media followers or, if you're publishing on other platforms, it's whoever reads your blog or website, listens to your podcast or watches your YouTube videos.

What's the story that you tell them?

Is it consistent?

Is it one you're proud of?

> **A great brand should reflect to the world the sum total of what it believes in, values and stands for.**

The world sees these beliefs and values, and those who feel the same way (or aspire to feel the same way) are drawn to that brand as if to a magnet.

Your professional personal brand works in exactly the same way.

If you consistently behave in a way that warmly showcases your beliefs and values, people will come to trust, respect and ultimately like you (which isn't necessarily the same as being 'popular' – people will like you for the right reasons).

> **And people like doing business with those they like.**
>
> **Boom.**

So, have you ever taken the time to work out what you stand for and value?

And how do you showcase this to the world?

You probably weren't taught at school or uni how to explore, define and communicate your values (Inga and I certainly weren't taught this). But this is a career hack that truly works and is integral to building your professional identity.

But remember, there's no point trying to manufacture a belief in something you don't really like in order to impress someone, or to win over your boss or client.

If it's not authentic to you, don't chase after it.

IF IT'S NOT *authentic* TO YOU, DON'T CHASE AFTER IT

HELP!

So I just threw a big one at you by asking you what you stand for and what you value.

Not sure how to work that out?

You're in luck.

> Now's the time to pick up your notebook.
>
> Write the heading 'My Values' at the top of a fresh page.
>
> The work you do in your notebook from chapters one and two will be the basis for all your learning from this book, so make sure you give yourself time to do it – your future self is thanking you already.

Why do values matter?

Once you know what you value and see as important, you will be able to decide how to act.

Your values give you clarity and focus and they'll help you improve in the areas of your life most important to you.

There are so many different roads you can take, so many places you can travel to.

But life is short – we only have a limited amount of time to explore, play, work and wander.

Many people dream of seeing and doing many things, while others only want to see a little but to see it very deeply and in great detail.

So imagine that as you move through life, everything around you is misty and shadowy. It's hard to see.

This is where your values come in. Like a bright light, they allow you to see a path ahead and to know which direction to move towards. And each step in this direction takes you closer to the very best life that you can choose for yourself.

This suddenly makes decision-making so simple and freeing – it's easy to decide how to act if you know what your values are.

How to choose your values:

> Turn back to your notebook and ask yourself two questions:
>
> What is the most important thing to me in life?
>
> What do I really want to achieve in my life?

Now just start writing. Think of this as a brainstorming session – there are no right or wrong answers. Be as detailed or as brief as you like.

Things you might list include: having a successful career, being in love, being healthy, having lots of money, exploring and going on adventures, having a family, being respected, having freedom and flexibility, feeling strong, being resourceful, spending time in nature, having fun, living in a big city, helping others, feeling secure, continuously learning, being happy, looking beautiful, fairness and justice.

This list could go on and on, but think honestly about your answers and whether they are truly important to you – no-one else, **just you**. There may be things you feel you *should* value, because of influence from family, friends or society, but I'd suggest not writing these down, because they're not intrinsic or authentic to you. If you try to live up to other people's values at the expense of your own, you won't be happy in the long run. If, for example, you really care about your family's or friends' opinions, this may mean that having great relationships is critical to you. So this is a value you could list instead.

Once you have come up with 10–20 things, shorten each one to one word – for example, being healthy would be 'health', having a successful career – whatever that might look like to you – would be 'success', having lots of money would be 'wealth' and having a family would simply be 'family'.

The next step is to prioritise your values.

Read through all your chosen values and pick out the most important one. To make this easier, ask yourself, 'If I could only have one of these things, would would it be?'

Then do this again with the answers that are left, until you have your second, third and fourth most important values, and so on.

By prioritising your values, you'll be able to rely on them when you need to make an important decision. If your health is the most important thing to you, it will be easier to say no to anything that takes you away from good health.

As an example, here are my current top ten values:

1. Health
2. Compassionate connection
3. Learning
4. Excellence
5. Freedom
6. Adventures
7. Kindness
8. Success
9. Contentment
10. Wealth.

It's important to note that my values have shifted slightly over the past year and are completely different to what they were ten years ago.

Five years ago, 'success' and 'wealth' were much higher on my list . . . and ten years ago, they were at the very top.

Where 'excellence' is, 'perfection' used to be. I learnt the hard way that perfection is an unachievable goal and that striving for it only made me disappointed and unhappy. But striving for excellence gives just as brilliant a result (and it's something you can actually achieve).

Where 'health' is now, 'beauty' was ten years ago. I'm the first to admit that I used to be pretty shallow and insecure; I would rather have been traditionally 'beautiful' – which at the time was to be thin, with clear, glowing skin and perfect hair, makeup, nails and clothes – than healthy. A lot of angst – eating disorders, anxiety and depression – taught me that this is a really dangerous and disempowering value to have. Now it's health all the way (and, ironically, since putting health first I've never felt more beautiful).

And this is the really exciting part about your values: they will change over time – whether subtly or drastically.

You may start out basing your values on those your parents taught you (or in complete opposition to these), but, later in life, decide that these values aren't for you.

Over time we each discover what works best for us, as we go through different stages of our lives and our experiences change us. And you get to decide what works best for you. You have no obligation to remain the same person – you can evolve however you choose.

> **So grab your diary and make a note to reassess your values in six months' time, and six months after that.**

These values will be a guiding light to you, especially when you need to make decisions, whether big or small. Simply ask yourself if the choice you're about to make upholds or compromises your values, then act accordingly.

We're going to come back to these values in later chapters, so keep them handy.

Your name is an important element of your personal brand.

If you don't already, learn to love it (or, if it's not going to cause significant harm, change it).

Be proud of it.

When you introduce yourself, use your name in full.

When you answer your phone, again, use your full name!

I've lost track of the number of young professionals – from recent graduates to those who've been in the industry for ten years – who don't bother to introduce themselves. And do you know what that means? No matter how smart or interesting that person is, I instantly forget them. And if I'm forgetting you, a potential boss or client is too.

My real name is Rebecca Brown.

As a kid, I was always called Becky.

When I moved to high school, I became Bec.

But when I was working in my first corporate gig, as I was about to walk into a meeting with a large financial firm, a very senior (and very old-school) director sniffed haughtily at my name.

'Bec? Really? Hmmph.'

I was then introduced as Rebecca Brown and, wanting to fit in, and deciding that they probably knew better than me, I didn't say anything. When my business cards arrived I saw that they'd also been changed to include my full name.

The problem was, I HATED being called Rebecca. I was never called it except when I was in trouble with my teachers or parents as a kid.

So every time my boss, colleagues or clients called me Rebecca, I felt really on edge.

I also felt like a fraud, as if I was playing a character (and, as I'm sure you know, when you're new to a job you already feel like a fraud because much of the time you have no idea what you're doing and are learning as you go).

I took Rebecca into my next job, thinking it was too late to change it. (Ahem – I was only two years in. It was a few more years until I realised that two years is a drop in the ocean.) I still hated being called Rebecca and wasn't getting used to it. People would call out 'Rebecca!' from across the room and I'd inadvertently ignore them because I had no idea they were referring to me.

Then one morning I had a meeting with a journalist.

We were both pretty happy – me because he'd run a huge story on one of our clients, and him because his by-line was staring up at us from the front page.

His name was a nightmare to both spell and pronounce. But he didn't care one bit, because it was who he was.

I looked at his name on the page and realised that I wasn't being true to myself. So when I walked back into the office that afternoon I rang IT and asked them to sort out a new bec@ email address for me.

I then emailed the whole company from that address to let them know about it.

My boss thought I'd gone a little mad, but it worked and, after a few weeks, no-one thought any more of it.

> Own who you are and the rest
> of the world will fall in line.

If your name is hard to pronounce, help people out so that they remember you:

- Tell them what it rhymes with when you introduce yourself.
- Put the phonetics in your email signature.
- Use it loud and proud on socials (with an accompanying video if you have to!).

Your CV.

Your CV is often the first impression prospective employers will get of who you are and what your personal brand is.

And putting yourself forward professionally in writing isn't as difficult as you might think.

If you're putting a CV together for a job in Australia, head to www.seek.com.au or www.careerone.com.au and check out their excellent advice.

Both sites recommend keeping it simple and succinct and tailoring it to the position that you're going for.

A tailored cover letter is also a must. The aim here is to sound like an actual human being, not a corporate robot. You want to show that you have thought about both the company's bigger picture and the day-to-day practicalities of the role you're going for, and to explain why you're interested in and the right fit for the company and this role. Don't use vague corporate jargon; be as clear and direct as possible. Write as you would speak, and try to keep your letter to a page. Then read it out loud – does it sound like a confident, professional and friendly version of you? Ask a friend or mentor who understands the tone you're going for to read it.

Focus on the WHY.

Sure, WHO you want to work with is important. I'm guessing you want to be with a great organisation, surrounded by interesting and clever people.

And WHAT you do and HOW you do it will be crucial. If you're not doing something you enjoy or you don't deliver, you won't get far in a role.

But if you can work out WHY you want to do all those things, this will drive all your other decisions.

For example, WHY do you want to work with interesting and clever people? Is it because they bring out your creativity, or because you thrive working in an inspiring and challenging environment?

WHY do you want to work for a great company? To push yourself to be your best? To prove to yourself that you're good at what you do? To earn a great income so that you can buy a house, travel or support a family? Because you love the idea of a company that aligns with your values? What else rings true for you?

It's also really important to communicate some of your WHYs to others – whether in your cover letter, CV, bio, LinkedIn profile or the 'About' page of your website.

When others can see your WHY, they can better understand what you value and what motivates you. This will help a prospective employer or potential client decide if you're going to be the right fit for them. And, importantly, once this line of communication is open, you'll be able to work out if *they're* the right fit for *you*.

The exception to the WHY rule relates to money. Reasons for wanting to earn a great income can be very personal and you therefore may not want to communicate them publicly or in early conversations. So keep this information to yourself until you've assessed the situation.

Establishing your style in design and life

Today my personal style is a big part of my brand, but I certainly didn't have it worked out from the start – it's something I've developed over time. As a designer, I can spend days looking at other people's work. Earlier in my career, I could be so influenced by someone else's design style that my work would begin to look similar to theirs. I'd pull bits and pieces from various people I admired, and eventually my work was looking really lost. There is a fine line between getting inspiration from other people's designs and trying to emulate their work. The mishmash of styles my work became may have replicated the best parts of those creatives I looked up to, but it certainly wasn't me.

> You have to find a style you are comfortable with – one that is, most importantly, YOURS.

By all means collate styles that you like. Put them in a folder on your computer, save them on Pinterest, or, if you prefer a tactile experience, go old-school and rip pages from magazines, use fabrics or materials, or print out things you see online. Then look for commonalities in the things you've chosen. Do this over time, with more and more examples selected. Can you start to see a pattern emerge that may inspire you to create your own style?

You will find that the more you experiment with and continually assess your style, to see if it feels true to you, the easier the work will become. It's a win-win. That said, there are of course trends within design, and it's good to stay current – but make sure your style doesn't get lost and rather sits side by side with what's 'of the moment'.

This principle can be applied not only to your design aesthetic but also to your personal wardrobe style. This is a lesson I wish I had learnt a long time ago, as it would have made my life a lot easier! Working in the magazine world, I would get so caught up with what was 'on trend' or how someone I admired in the office dressed. When shopping I would think, 'What would they buy?' This left me with a closet full of choices but none that really expressed my individual style.

Work out what you feel comfortable with and go with it. The fewer choices you have, the simpler and less stressful it is to get dressed each day. People will recognise you for you. The biggest lesson is realising that you are your own amazing person with your own unique style. As well as being a time and money saver, when you're wearing clothes you feel confident and happy in, you'll automatically do better at work.

A lot of uber successful creatives have a uniform – take a look at Matilda Kahl, an art director at Saatchi & Saatchi, who created a uniform for herself after realising that her male colleagues didn't face the same 'what on earth am I going to wear' stress every morning. She chose a white silk shirt and black dress pants and bought multiple pairs of each so she could rotate them without having to do laundry every day. She added a black leather bow around the collar, and, if it's cold, she throws on a blazer.

While I don't have a strict work uniform, I've also adopted a minimalist's mindset and have chosen not to have an extensive wardrobe. My go-to outfit is usually a striped or plain top paired with blue or black jeans, pumps and a cool blazer. In the warmer months, I tend to wear striped or single-colour short shift dresses. I've found that if I go for anything too patterned I get sick of it quickly, and people are also more likely to notice that I'm repeating an outfit. That said, if I'm going out in the evening or to a special lunch, I love a bit of leopard print. I find that if I stick to what I like and feel confident and comfortable in, there's less decision fatigue and getting ready is so much quicker and easier. And that leaves me with more time and in a better headspace to do all the other things I love.

Style suggestions

- Make thoughtful, considered purchases. Do you LOVE it, or do you just like it?
- Know what looks good on you and stick to it (though this isn't to say you can't experiment with different styles). Fewer decisions = more time.
- Less is more – choose quality pieces that you can mix and match. 'Sustainable is the new black' so feel good about wearing the same garment often.
- Try to make trending items only 10 per cent of your wardrobe. This will not only save you money but will also allow you to have fun with the latest fashions and accessories without running out of 'classic', timeless go-to pieces. Only update your trend pieces when you feel the previous ones have really lost their lustre or are looking dated.

And remember . . .

Your style and your brand, like your life, are *yours*.

'Authenticity' is a word that's a bit overused these days, but that doesn't make it any less important.

Developing your own personal brand can be fun because it will evolve with you over time – it's never static so never boring.

And it's worth investing your time and energy in because it's closely linked to your career progression and professional reputation, which will grow stronger over time the more consistent you are.

In addition, the confidence that comes when you're comfortable with who you are and what you do is priceless.

So develop your authenticity, think it, act it, and own it.

CHAPTER 2

SUCCESS

how it's different for everyone, why you need to define what it means to you, and how to measure and continually assess it

The word 'success' gets thrown around a lot. But what does it really mean? We'll get to that shortly, but what's really exciting is that the sooner you discover what your personal measure of success is, the happier you'll be.

And it's okay if your measure of success changes from time to time – nothing in life stays the same forever and that's a great thing.

Just make sure that you're true to your own measure of success, no-one else's.

Constantly striving to compete with someone who has a different idea of success to you is like running the 400-metre hurdles in the Olympics when you're supposed to be in the 100-metre swimming finals. You can't and won't win.

So how do you work out what your definition of success is?

We're going to do that here, in four steps.

Step one is identifying your values, which we covered in chapter one, so TICK.

Step two is discovering your passions.

What are your passions?

> Grab your notebook and, across three different pages, write these questions as headings:
>
> 1. What do I enjoy doing?
> 2. What am I really good at?
> 3. What would I *like* to be really good at?

Now, under these three headings, write down EVERYTHING you can think of. Be super honest with yourself, as this list is just for you.

Here are some pointers:

1. What do I enjoy doing?

These are things that make you feel content, energised, excited, proud, accomplished or simply happy. Perhaps time slips away when you're doing these things because you love them so much.

You might include: reading, writing, planning parties, attending parties, making conversation, listening, cooking, watching TV, spending time with large groups of people, spending time with small groups of people, being in nature, being around small children, being around older people, serving others, working for a charity, running, swimming, hiking, making videos, making podcasts, coding, doing someone's hair, doing someone's make-up, drawing, painting, teaching, singing, or taking photos. Jot down whatever it is YOU love to do.

If you're struggling here, think back to what you naturally gravitated towards when you were a kid. Often people have intrinsic loves that stay with them from the time they were very small.

For example, when I was about eleven years old, I opened a 'restaurant' for my parents and siblings. Growing up on a farm, miles from anywhere, we didn't have the luxury of eating out very often. So on weekends, I'd get out my textas and design a menu, and become a restaurateur, chef, waiter and dish pig all at once. I doubt my restaurant would have been a commercial success as I charged about a dollar per person, but I can see now that from a young age I've enjoyed creating experiences and events that give people a moment to remember – a passion that has carried through to my business today, as I help our clients create memorable brand experiences for their customers, audiences and other stakeholders. My signature Bec Brown Brownies were also no doubt born from these weekends spent cooking and baking as a kid.

So what new ideas are coming up for you now? Write them all down.

2. What am I really good at?

This isn't what you think you MIGHT be good at, but what you actually ARE good at right now. Be honest – this list will probably be shorter than the first (or, who knows, it may even be longer!). Again, list everything that comes to mind.

3. What would I *like* to be really good at?

These are things you're not yet great at but are willing to put in the hard yards to master. Be REALLY honest about this too – you might really like singing, for example, but are you willing to find a teacher and put in time and money for weekly or even twice-weekly lessons on top of doing at least an hour of practice every day?

Some of these things will be obvious to you; others you'll need to think more deeply about. Have you received encouraging feedback about a particular skill at work or school?

Your list might include creative skills, such as drawing, styling or make-up artistry; skills in other fields, such as sport, law, coding, medicine or wellness; or soft skills, such as being organised, calm under pressure, or great at problem-solving.

Now that you've completed all three lists, go through them and highlight the things that appear in both list one and two as well as those that appear in both list one and three.

Then consider the following question:

> If you had all the money in the world and didn't need to worry about it ever again, what would you spend your life doing?

Take a look at your highlighted list – does it come close to your answer to this question?

Some people will complete this exercise and instantly realise what they love and where their passions lie. Maybe it's working with animals, campaigning for social change, being around kids, helping the sick, finding a cure for illness, or travelling the world.

Maybe you want to run a hugely profitable company.

Maybe you want to go shopping every day, eat at fine-dining restaurants, and get massages and beauty treatments.

Maybe you want to practise law.

Maybe you want to become famous.

Know that there's no right or wrong answer.

If you are still looking blankly at your page and don't feel passionate about any of these things, there's one final step you can take: follow your curiosity.

Sometimes you won't feel passionate about much at all, and that's okay. But I bet you're curious about something – so, as a last resort, vow to follow that curiosity instead.

By pursuing your curiosity, you'll keep moving and experiencing new things. Without it, you'll remain stationary, stuck in a rut.

So if you're not madly passionate about anything, what are you curious about?

Now you've worked out what your values and passions (or curiosities) are, **step three:**

> **Grab your notebook and answer the following DREAM LIFE questions.**

These questions will help you decide if your definition of success is sustainable and will make you happy. Because if it's not and it won't, what is the point?

Ask yourself: If I concentrated on my values and followed my passions or curiosities:

1. Would I be content?
2. Would I still have time to immerse myself in other things that bring me joy? (For example, if you want to run a hugely profitable company or practise law in a big firm, are you prepared to let go of many of your other passions for a little while, given the amount of work and time it will take to establish your own company or become a lawyer?)
3. Would I be a nice human being, someone who's good to others and to myself?

Take all the time you need to think about this. There's no hurry.

There are high achievers who make a lot of money, who regularly appear on TV as experts in their field and who have huge social media followings. They may have all the finer things in life – a luxury house, an expensive car, designer clothes. They may have a partner and children. They may take exotic vacations.

To many people, this probably looks like success. And that high achiever may also consider themselves successful – that's up to them.

But I've learnt that often people who seem to have it all, deep down, are not that happy.

And while we may think they're successful, they possibly don't see themselves that way.

They might feel there is always more to achieve, so they struggle to feel content or satisfied, or they might depend on those around them for constant validation.

I know this not only from observing and talking to others, but also because, for a brief period of time, that was me. Mostly due to seeking external validation, I'd drifted away from my own values and passions.

And we've seen countless times the world over that achieving for the sake of achievement without thought to your values – perhaps with a belief that the end always justifies the means – constantly needing external validation, and being so busy 'achieving' that there's no time left for quality relationships is a never-ending treadmill of exhausting, relentless pain.

> Ask yourself, as I had to ask myself, is this a treadmill you want to get on?
>
> What will it cost you to 'achieve' and own all these things?

If you're not prepared to pay, maybe it's time to re-evaluate.

> Now, on a fresh page in your notebook, write yourself a short summary.
>
> My personal definition of success right now is . . .

Step four – now that you have a definition of success that feels right for *you*, let's talk about how to progress towards that goal and how to measure your progress along the way.

You're going to write down all the things you want to achieve, both in the next six months and in the next three years.

This is a vitally important step, as numerous studies have shown that you are anywhere from 45 to 80 per cent more likely to achieve your goals if you write them down. And I can tell you now – it works. The more you do it, the better the result will be. Every year when I review my goals and work out what percentage of them I've achieved, the number goes up. It's both satisfying and motivating.

So, create a table across a couple of fresh pages and split it into categories. These five are a good start:

Category	Six months	Accountability	Three years	Accountability
Work				
Personal				
Family & friends				
Health				
Financial				

Make each goal SMART – Specific, Measurable, Actionable, Realistic and Timely.

Specific and Realistic: Be clear about exactly what you want to do and make sure it's realistically acheivable. Instead of 'get healthy by next week', you could write 'feel more energised by the end of this month by going to bed by 10 pm each night, going to yoga three times a week, eating more whole foods and only consuming one sugary treat a week, one coffee a day and avoiding booze.'

Measurable and Actionable: The accountability column is where you write how you'll know if you've achieved your goal and also how you will stay on track to achieving it. If you want to learn how to play guitar, for example, write down the steps you'll take – research what guitar you'll get, who your teacher will be, how many lessons you'll have, how many times a week you'll practise and when you'll practise. If your ultimate goal is to release videos on YouTube or social media, write down the date you want to start posting those videos, because that deadline will help you stay on track with your practice. Also estimate how many hours in total each task will take and break that total down into daily or weekly instalments, which you can document separately in your diary or planner (if you don't already have one, it's time to get one and start using it!).

Timely: Be realistic about the amount of time you'll need to spend on each goal. Saving a deposit for a new home is unlikely to take you six months, so that would probably go in the three years column. In contrast, if you're focused on getting into shape by maintaining a healthier lifestyle with regular exercise and a sustainable eating plan, you'll certainly be able to see a result within six months. If you're just starting out in your career, working towards being your own boss would likely go in the three years column. And when you estimate how long something will take you, give yourself some buffer time. Otherwise, if unexpected events get in the way and you hit the six-month mark without having achieved your goal, you might feel discouraged and give up. So give yourself a few extra weeks or months as needed – but don't allow too much extra time, as you need to keep some pressure on yourself to actually get it done.

Stay on track

Once you've completed this table, look at it every day. Along with your definition of personal success, stick this table to your wall or pin-up board or put it in your diary. If you really want to achieve these things, put it by your bed or stick it to your bathroom mirror too. You need to be reminded of your goals and they'll also help you with decision-making. If a new opportunity arises, ask yourself: will it help or hinder your goals? If it's a great opportunity and you want to take it, which of these things are you willing to push back?

Now, admittedly (and embarrassingly), back when I was twenty-three, my top financial goal was to save enough money to buy a black Mercedes SLK-Class convertible (the one with indicators in the side mirrors that was cutting-edge at the time). My main health goal was to be a consistent size zero (which was clearly not about health, and you have no idea how ridiculous that goal was given my natural body type). And my career goal was to be performing on Broadway with a record deal in the works. Social media as we know it was still several years away (though my MySpace page was going off), but if it had been around at the time I know I would have wanted hundreds of thousands of followers. I don't think I even had any personal or family & friends goals because I was too busy frantically trying to lock down the others.

There's nothing wrong with dreaming big but clearly my idea of what constitutes a beautiful life has dramatically changed since my early twenties.

What I didn't do at the time was ask myself this critical question: would I be happy doing the things it'd take to achieve these goals? The end result sounded brilliant, but what about the journey there?

If I had asked myself this question, I would have saved myself a lot of heartache.

At the time, I certainly wasn't happy. I had an eating disorder, was a fickle friend and family member, was plagued by frequent bouts of anxiety and depression, and was binge drinking on weekends to try to block it all out.

I also didn't stop to consider if I'd actually be happy when I'd 'made it'. But the honest answer would have been no.

I was a bit of a late bloomer in terms of carving out a happy, sustainable, fulfilling life, and it wasn't until my late twenties that I began to work out what truly mattered. Asking myself the three DREAM LIFE questions was a good start.

So how do you keep on track to success?

First you assess it.

Keep coming back to the table you've created. Use a diary or planner that allows you to have both a weekly to-do list and a daily one. That satisfaction of crossing things off your list will become addictive.

Life will always have unexpected twists and turns so accommodate these as you go, but also try to anticipate what might happen over the next few months that could help or hinder your progress.

A very wise friend once said this to me:

Every time you respond to a person or situation; every time you do something; and every time you don't do something (i.e. you procrastinate), you should ask yourself:

> Am I currently behaving in a way that is towards my greater good?

Your greater good is the 'you' you truly want to be – the 'you' that is healthy and happy, pursuing your values, passions or curiosities, and leading the successful life that you've defined.

If the answer is 'no', then do something else.

If the answer is 'yes', then keep going (and give yourself a high five for being such a star).

If the answer is 'I don't know what my greater good is anymore – I don't even know if I ever knew what it was,' then go back to the start and work out what your values are and whether they pass the DREAM LIFE test.

How do you make sure your success is satisfying?

Warning: the answer is going to sound clichéd.

But the thing about clichés is that there's usually a ton of truth to them.

So here it is:

> Real personal success will never solely be a destination. It will always include the journey towards an end goal.

I'm sure you know that the satisfaction you get from achieving a goal can be very fleeting. But looking back at all the fantastic moments on your journey there can make you feel incredibly proud.

Just make sure you take the time to celebrate smashing one of your goals and to appreciate how far you've come. After all your hard work, you deserve to celebrate that journey's conclusion.

And now you've reached the fun stage – setting your next goal.

INGA'S TIPS

It's good to remember that there is no finish line – imaginary or otherwise. You won't wake up one day and think, 'This is it, I have arrived!'

You are going to have many goals throughout your life, and you move from one to the next as you grow and develop as a person.

And as you're doing this, you need to know deep down that, for as long as you're alive, you'll keep moving forward. This is what keeps life interesting.

Think evolution, not revolution.

So settle in and enjoy the ride.

And at the risk of sounding like a reality TV show contestant . . . it really is all about the journey.

CHAPTER 3

HOW TO GET NOTICED

in a positive, authentic way

We live in a competitive, attention-grabbing world.

And attention is currency. It's valuable.

Any professional business or brand needs attention to survive (let alone thrive).

Before the rise of tech and social media, adults had a smaller number of people in their lives, and events outside their local community were communicated to them by mail or the media. But thanks to the internet, and especially social media, the number of people we 'encounter' in our lives has increased exponentially, from hundreds to tens of thousands, and we have the potential to reach millions more.

And this isn't something our brains are equipped for.

We simply don't have the capacity to remember all the people who cross our paths.

So what does this mean for us?

Professionally, we want to be noticed – ideally in a positive way, and for behaving authentically.

The saying 'where focus goes, energy flows' applies here.

> **When your boss or your client's focus is on you (for good reasons), you are more likely to be promoted or to work together again.**

This chapter gives you some tried-and-true tactics for combating focus fatigue and for attracting the attention you're after.

But first, let's quickly rule out the type of attention we're NOT working towards:

1. Have you heard the saying 'the squeaky wheel gets the grease' or 'whoever shouts loudest, wins'?

   This is the idea that if you're 'noisy' enough – in terms of volume, colour, size or repetition – people will focus on you.

   The problem with this idea is that often very little thought is put into what's actually said or done. There's quantity but not enough quality. A lot of smoke and mirrors, not a lot of substance.

And once your audience – your boss, colleagues or customers – realise this, they'll switch off faster than a light in a blackout. And regaining their attention and trust will be incredibly difficult. (Plus, let's not forget that, over time, noisy things become very annoying!)

2. Do you think that the happiest, most self-secure and truly successful people in the world ever look online and think to themselves, 'Wow, I'm going to have to show more skin. Time to get my gear off and flash it across social media.'

   I don't know about you, but **I'd rather earn respect than get short-lived attention**.

   Now don't get me wrong, I'm ALL for body positivity. We each have the right to feel comfortable and happy in our own skin, and to dress how we feel. And if showing off your body either naked or clothed is how you choose to creatively express yourself, go for it.

   But too often this is done from a place of insecurity, for validation or attention based purely on sex appeal or looks, rather than more important things, such as what is said and done and how we treat others. If relying solely on attention from others based on how we look is what's driving us, it's going to start to feel pretty empty, pretty fast.

So here's an alternative.

To **get the dream job, to land the lucrative and lovely client** – hell, to even just **attract beautiful people into your life** – here are **four simple things** you can do:

1. Be someone others can trust – have integrity, and always be honest, ethical and well-mannered. And remember, it's always better to under-promise and over-deliver than to over-promise and under-deliver.
2. Be clear – communicate transparently and consistently in a way that's always on-brand for you – whether in person, via email, on social media or in reports.
3. Provide solutions – in a professional environment, everyone wants a solution to their problem, so never underestimate the power of the person who humbly offers an idea or action to solve an unwanted challenge. Rather than arriving with a list of reasons why something won't work, think of an alternative. If you truly think something won't work, say so but provide other options. And if you don't have a solution, use the word 'yet'. As in, 'I don't know how we're going to do that . . . yet. Let me come back to you.' Then make sure you follow through.
4. Demonstrate your value – constantly and gently remind those you work for of what you give to them and the business, and suggest or show them what else you can do.

These four things are not only the foundation for long-lasting attention, which will help you to stay professionally competitive, but will also allow you to build an outstanding reputation.

It's worth considering how can you incorporate more of these things into your daily life.

Another one that rates a mention when you're trying to get noticed in a positive way – and there's no sugary way to say this so I'm going to be blunt:

Try to avoid having resting bitch face.

If you have a naturally sunny disposition, good for you (and good for everyone else who benefits from the warmth and positivity that you no doubt bring to those around you).

I'D RATHER
EARN
respect
THAN GET
SHORT-LIVED
ATTENTION

If you don't, there's absolutely nothing wrong with that. There are certainly times when I don't want to smile, and when my neutral face looks downright murderous. Sometimes we don't even realise that our natural 'at rest' faces look negative, because we tend to instantly change our expression when we see ourselves in the mirror. It's easy to say, 'It's not my fault if people choose to think something about me based on how I naturally act. Everyone else can just suck it up, I'm being ME.'

Yes – and no.

Yes, how others choose to think is not your concern. And spending your life trying to change other people's ideas will be a never-ending battle. You do you.

But you are still responsible for the image that you project to the world. And if the people who meet you misinterpret a blank expression as a sneer, and go away thinking you're negative, some of that is on you.

> **Keep in mind that, ultimately, people want to be heard and understood and have their problems solved.**

If you can do this consistently, calmly and with a better attitude than anyone else, you're going to get that promotion or keep that client.

I've come across many people who are great problem-solvers– from staff who cheerfully tackle daily challenges, to contractors who always go above and beyond everything they've promised, to journalists who are transparent, honest and open to others' ideas. Not only do I remember them, I make an effort to reward, promote or recommend them, to continue doing business with them and to keep them in my life.

When I was working at Universal Music in my late twenties, I'd set up album and tour promotions for famous international artists with radio shows. The artist would come in for an interview about their new album and tour, answer questions from their fans in the audience – a hundred listeners who'd won tickets to meet their favourite star – and, when the live show had finished, do meet and greets, photos and signings.

Needless to say, these events, while always a lot of fun, were notoriously unpredictable, and a lot of detailed planning went into them. One particular artist I managed didn't do them often, and I'd really had to fight hard to make the event happen. The artist was in Sydney for a week and I was responsible for more than fifty interviews and media events in his promotional schedule. I was also working with ten other artists that month, so, as you can imagine, time was scant.

While it sounds like I'm setting up to tell a horror story, on this particular morning everything ran like a dream. Our artist was in a great and generous mood, the interview was friendly and funny, the fans were awestruck, and the promotional messages couldn't have been delivered better.

I worked hard all morning like the proverbial duck – smoothly manoeuvring, smiling and calm on the surface, while at the same time paddling furiously to keep the whole thing afloat – and the end result was that the artist, radio station and fans were happy.

I didn't think much about the event until I received an email later that week from the big, BIG boss at Universal. It was a forwarded email and he'd copied in my boss and several other senior execs within the company. He had just written, 'Take a bow Bec, well done.'

I scrolled to the very bottom of the email chain and saw that after the radio event, the executive producer of the show had emailed *her* boss to say she'd just had the best experience and had namechecked me as the reason it'd gone so well. Her boss then forwarded the email to *his* boss, who then forwarded it to Universal's President of Australasia, saying the same thing.

Suddenly I was getting noticed. And yes, this really, REALLY helped my career.

So what had I done well that morning?

I'd worked hard with management to get the artist to agree to the event – which **provided a solution** for the radio station.

I'd been really transparent and detailed in all my emails and calls regarding the set-up – I'd used **clear communication**.

I delivered on everything I said I would, which made the executive producer **trust me**.

After the event, I made it clear that I'd love to work with her again, and mentioned that it was great the station's listeners were so happy – which **reminded her of my value**.

And even though there were stressful moments throughout the process, I acted calmly and cheerfully.

Now I certainly didn't set out to get noticed that morning – I was simply trying to do my job to the best of my ability. But I wouldn't have received the recognition I did if I'd not followed the above four rules.

A sidenote: what goes around comes around. Ever since that email was sent about me (by that kind executive producer who, unsurprisingly, has gone on to have great career success), I've tried to give credit and call out excellent work when I see it, both to the person who's done the work and to their boss or senior stakeholders. This is a great way to show appreciation and creates a kinder and more constructive work environment.

PROVIDE solutions

YES versus NO

At the start of your career, as you're learning and developing, learn to say 'yes' a lot.

The condition is that you need to review your personal values first.

Can't see any compromises? Then move ahead. Who knows what this opportunity may lead to!

The more opportunities you say yes to, the more people you meet and work with, the more experience you gain, the more people will notice you. This also shows senior execs that you can step up and take on more responsibility. All these things give rise to the kind of positive attention you want.

And on your career journey, don't ever feel frustrated or worried if you need to take a short-term job in an industry that's not where you want to end up. Everyone has to make a living somehow, so do what you need to do, but keep your eye on the prize.

While I was studying music in my teens and early twenties, I worked at KFC, McDonald's (the Drive-Thru was my favourite), at a sandwich shop, at a cafe, behind the bar at a pub, as a barista and waitress at an Italian fine-dining restaurant, and as a receptionist at a car dealership. While these weren't my dream jobs, they paid for my rent, car, food and other spending, and, importantly, taught me very early on how to best work with other people and care for customers. That's an education that's hard to beat. I always made it clear to my potential employers that I had this kind of experience too, because it demonstrated my value.

However, at some stage in your career, there will come a time when you need to start saying 'no' a lot more, or, at least, 'not right now'.

The reason for this is that, over time, you will develop a much stronger sense of your purpose and what you want to do with your life. And to do what you want to do well will require dedicated focus, so you'll do fewer things in order to excel in the areas you've chosen.

By narrowing your focus, you'll strengthen your expertise. And with expertise comes attention, as others will seek you out for the service that only you or your company can provide.

But the condition here is to remain open-minded and flexible, as tunnel vision can shut out great ideas, shortcuts and amazing opportunities.

Earn trust, communicate clearly, provide solutions and demonstrate your value.

CHAPTER 4

MEETINGS

dos and don'ts

There are so many types of meetings:

- casual one-on-one coffee catch-ups
- team brainstorming sessions
- working lunches
- after-work drinks
- industry events
- conference and video calls
- huge boardroom meetings that seem to involve half the company (don't even get me started on the ones where no-one really knows why they're there, or ones that could have been sorted out with a phone call or email. These days, if a meeting doesn't have a clear agenda, I'm outta there. But back to the point . . .).

No matter the kind, all meetings follow the same pattern:

1. You arrive.
2. You discuss.
3. You reach some kind of conclusion.
4. You leave.

Depending on who is in attendance, each meeting has its own etiquette. And this isn't usually something that's taught. Often people pick this up from experience, or take their cue from the meeting host or the most senior person there.

But without being too dramatic, the way you handle yourself in a meeting can make or break your career.

Consider that an exciting thing because, as we discussed in chapter three, this is an opportunity for you to get noticed and to build your professional image.

Here are some dos and don'ts. These should be tweaked to suit the style of the meeting – a casual coffee catch-up is hardly going to resemble a huge boardroom affair chaired by the CEO, but the principles remain the same.

> You want to appear credible and in control and for all parties to leave feeling satisfied that they have achieved something.

DO:

- **Your homework** – make sure you've read any pre-meeting material and have done your research on the topic. If you're meeting new people, look them up on LinkedIn or other social media platforms beforehand so that you know what they look like and understand their background.
- **Introduce yourself** to anyone you haven't previously met. Use your full name and, in some cases, mention your job title and what you actually do. Practise this in front of a mirror if you need to.
- **Put your phone away** and ensure it's on silent (not on vibrate). Unless you need to use it to refer to something during the meeting, keep it off the table and in your bag or pocket. And if you do need it during the meeting, use it for that moment then put it back away again. Doing these things shows that you respect the person or people you're meeting with and that you're fully present. In today's busy world, giving someone your attention can mean a great deal to them, and you'll be well-remembered for it.
- **Contribute early**, but only after you've listened to others and really know what's going on. Come prepared with one or two points to offer so that you are visible early on.
- **Sit near the influencers.** Don't tentatively take a seat right up the back of the room – if you're going to be in the game, you need to physically be there! Keep in mind there may be a hierarchy in a room full of execs though, so perhaps don't sit right next to the CEO if the CFO, COO and CMO are all there too. But be present near the key players.
- **Listen.** Actually listen to what other people are saying, rather than just thinking about what you're going to say next.
- **Reframe what the other person has said** to make sure you understand them correctly ('So I'm hearing that the results from the last campaign were great in this area, but you're unhappy with this section, right?').
- **Buy yourself some time** with phrases such as 'That's a really interesting point' or 'I'm glad you brought that up' if you need to pause and collect your thoughts before replying.

- **Have an opinion.** Be firm and bold – that's why you're there. But make sure your opinion is solution-oriented and can be backed up with facts.
- **Be respectful** of other people's time and opinions.
- **Use your body language** to show that you're present. Focus your attention outwards and use eye contact.
- **If a meeting has become heated** and more and more people are speaking loudly or aggressively, **speak more quietly when it's your turn to speak. But do so with real precision**, making eye contact with those you're talking to. People will need to lean in to hear you. This is one of the best tricks I've learnt as it brings the energy in the room back to a better place and stops the shouting and grandstanding.
- **Follow up afterwards.** This might be by sending the meeting attendees a short email thanking them for their time and providing follow-up information or letting them know that you're on the case.
- **Send an email to say thank you** if someone has bought you lunch or drinks. If it was your shout, still follow up and thank them for their time.

DON'T:

- **Be late.** Allow enough time so that you arrive at the meeting feeling organised and unrushed. If you're going to someone's office and need to let reception know you're there so they can call them, only do this a few minutes before your meeting. Don't have the receptionist call them fifteen minutes early as they probably have other things to do and are going to feel unduly pressured by your schedule.
- **Check emails or texts** on your phone during the meeting – it is SO rude. If you're expecting a critical call or message that the rest of the people at the meeting will understand is a huge priority, start the meeting by letting them know about this and apologising in advance. Explain that they have your full attention and that you'd rather be there with them, but that you may need to take the call or reply to the message in an emergency.
- **Have negative body language** – don't cross your arms, roll your eyes or turn your back on anyone you're with.
- **Sit on the fence or use indecisive language** if you have a real opinion either way, such as 'whatever', 'I guess' or 'I dunno . . . maybe.'
- **Finish people's sentences.** Feel free to nod and agree with them as they're talking, but let them say what they want to say. When you finish other people's sentences they don't feel heard. This can also come across as quite patronising.
- **Always have to have the last word.** Make sure you've given other people an ample opportunity to speak.

And if you're still feeling a little meh about the whole meeting thing, whether from nerves or boredom, revert to the oldest and most effective trick in the book: fake it till you make it.

Act like you're an attentive and confident person, and you soon will be.

You wouldn't be at this point in your career and at this type of meeting if you couldn't handle it.

Be brave. You've got this.

ACT LIKE YOU'RE AN

attentive & confident

PERSON & YOU SOON WILL BE

Conference and video calls

Ugh. Let's be honest. These things can be painful.

From bad connections to not knowing who's talking, to background noise and more.

For a truly excellent laugh, watch the YouTube video 'Tripp Crosby: A conference call in real life'. In just over three minutes, it'll show you all the things you want to try and avoid during a phone conference call.

On a call you obviously don't have the luxury of visual cues, so your tone of voice becomes much more important.

Think about that for a second – do you know how you sound? Have you ever recorded yourself and played this back? What's the background noise? That's all anyone is hearing. But don't worry – chapter six will help you to make sure your voice is working its best for you.

If you're in a noisy environment, put your phone on mute and quickly switch it back on when you're talking.

And while you don't want to talk over others, if someone has just finished saying something, remember to give them a response. Even just 'got it', or 'that makes sense, thank you'. Otherwise the other person will feel ignored or as if they're talking into thin air and you'll get the famous 'hello, hello . . . are you still there?' from them.

You also need to make sure that people know who's talking. Aside from introducing yourself or being introduced at the start of the call, make sure you identify yourself each time you speak. It's as simple as stating, 'It's Bec here, I wanted to say that . . .' If you're in a big meeting with multiple companies in attendance, you could potentially assign one person to speak from each group.

Video calls are less problematic but there's still bound to be a tech issue, so be patient. There will no doubt be annoying awkward moments during the call. Someone's video may freeze, or there may be lots of background noise. If the host hasn't already pointed this out, feel free to mention it. But don't laugh at someone's frozen frame (seriously, no-one likes to be laughed at), and set a time limit for dealing with the tech. If everyone's not on the call within ten minutes, agree to revert to a phone conference call instead. The day is ticking away and, frankly, life's too short.

Working lunches or after-work drinks

These can be really fun but deserve their own section because they're out of the office and have their own special rules.

Each event will differ, but the general etiquette is that you follow the lead of the host or the most senior person there. Alternatively, if you are the host, you create an environment that makes your guests feel comfortable and well treated.

The host always picks up the bill, and the guests always thank the host.

If alcohol is served and you want to drink, take it very easy. I know of countless situations where talented people have lost their hard-earned professional reputations thanks to one too many drinks at a work event. So have one or two drinks if you want to but then switch to a sparkling water or mocktail. Own your decision. And it goes without saying, never drink and drive.

While some companies have a 'work hard, play hard' mentality, they are becoming more and more old school, simply because we're now more enlightened. Smart companies are moving towards providing their teams with a sustainable career that doesn't entail a poor work–life balance (or trying to work through a hideous hangover). Remember that you're under no obligation to drink at all or to drink as much as anyone else at the event is. Allow everyone there to do their own thing, and you do yours.

We have a rule at The Comms Department that none of us will ever be, or even appear to be, the 'DP' – that's the Drunk Publicist – at work events. And this has meant that we've retained our excellent professional reputation.

Events

These technically aren't meetings but they're still work functions so you need to be mindful of the etiquette. The same rules apply here about minimising alcohol and being a good guest or host.

There's so much advice out there about this, but it's up to you to work out what you think is right. If you need some pointers, googling 'how to be a good host' or 'business etiquette for corporate events' will give you plenty to work with.

When I first started out, I used to feel quite intimidated walking into industry events. Everyone looked like they knew each other and people were already in groups. I felt so much like an outsider.

I'd watch my boss expertly manoeuvre around the room and I'd think, 'How does she do that?' It looked like she had it all together and that it just came naturally to her.

I'll be the first to admit, too, that I thought having a glass of champagne might help to settle my nerves. Sometimes one glass did help. Though I later discovered that I was more focused and in control without it.

After talking to my old boss about this years later, I realised she didn't have it all together. But through experience she had learnt what to do.

What I took from my conversation with her was that **I needed to be prepared, and to be bold**. At most of the meetings she attended there were many people she didn't know and she'd simply walk up to them, introduce herself and start talking. A lot of this came down to preparation – she'd take the time before an event to work out who would be there. She'd then think about what they had in common, either personally or professionally, that she could talk to them about.

This second tip was also a gamechanger.

I had this saying on the pin-up board in my office for years:

> **Feeling nervous?**
>
> **Be of service.**

This mindset makes approaching people so much easier as you've moved from simply talking to them, to *helping them*.

What can you bring to a conversation that may help that person? The details of a business contact? An idea for a story for their publication? A recommendation for a hot new restauarant that you think they'd like? All of this comes back to being prepared – you need to know what this person needs or wants. And if you don't know this in advance, you can find out in general conversation. Ask them questions about themselves or their business and you'll soon find out what excites them. I also use this approach when I'm pitching an idea to a journalist or client – it's much less scary when you know that you're helping them.

And if you're still feeling apprehensive, before you go in, take a moment somewhere quiet – perhaps the bathroom or your car – to close your eyes and take a few deep breaths and concentrate on good feelings such as being safe, strong, calm and happy. When you rehearse these feelings, your brain's neurons get used to activating them, so when the time comes to call upon them in 'real' situations, they're more easily accessible.

INGA'S TIPS

Something that I had to learn while working in magazines was how to distinguish between socialising and actual work.

I was lucky enough to work with an amazing group of like-minded, creative and fun people, many of whom have become lifelong friends.

But, wow, was it easy to let a meeting go off track. We'd start talking about a problem with that month's issue and, innocently enough, discuss one of the celebrity feature articles – then, rather than talking about the work that needed to be done on that article, we'd descend into a gossip session. This would turn into an all-in on everyone's dating and love lives, and suddenly an hour had passed and we still hadn't found a solution to the problem! Then we all had to work late or on the weekend and were stressed out of our heads.

So set boundaries – during work hours, keep it about work. At lunch or after work, relax and enjoy each other's fabulous stories.

This leads to my next point, about how to rein in a meeting when it gets out of hand.

Firstly, have an agenda. If you call a meeting, this is your responsibility.

Either before the meeting or as the meeting starts, ask everyone there if there's anything you need to add to the agenda.

Map out a rough timeline and allocate five, ten or fifteen minutes for each point. Ideally this should also be done prior to the meeting, but if there's no time, do it at the start. You may realise that there's no way you can cover everything you want to in that time, so tackle the most time-sensitive and important points first.

If someone else has called the meeting, they may have already sent around an agenda beforehand. If not, ask them what is on it. If they don't have one, under the guise of being helpful and making sure they're able to cover everything they want to, offer to create one on the spot.

Bec here again: I love this. And let me tell you, this is something you always need to be aware of.

My team members have become some of my best friends, and it'd be so easy to stop and socialise if we weren't disciplined. When we have whole-team meetings, we use the timer on our phones (or a kitchen timer, when we're having no-phone meetings) to set intervals to work to. This means that we can go all-in and get really detailed and creative in our discussions without having to worry if we're going over time, because the alarm will go off and catch us. It's like a (really chirpy) safety net.

credible AND IN CONTROL

CHAPTER 5

SOCIAL MEDIA

dos and don'ts

I love social media.

But only because I understand it.

And I have rules around how I use it.

Rule number 1: Remember that it's not real.

Whatever someone chooses to post, whether it's a heavily filtered photo, an 'I'm so raw this is all me' video, or a microblog of personal musings, it's still curated.

And what's a curator? Someone who chooses what people should see.

> So never compare.
>
> But also try not to judge.

Rule number 2: Try to be mindful and deliberate when you use it.

Social media is a tool. And you get to decide how you use that tool.

The saying goes, 'Tools make great servants but terrible masters.'

So will you allow social media to be your servant or your master?

Studies have shown that the longer people spend on social media, the more likely it is that they'll leave in a negative mood, regardless of how they were feeling to begin with.

There are a few reasons for this:

- You're procrastinating. Scrolling through your socials is easier than doing that important task you're supposed to be working on. But then you feel worse for not having done it, and maybe more stressed because now you have less time to complete it.
- The longer you're on social media, the more likely you are to end up mindlessly scrolling, and you have no real choice over the content that's placed in front of you, which is both disempowering and can mess with your already-busy brain as it attempts to take in a lot of random or irrelevant info. Sure, you choose who you follow, but you can't really control what appears in your feed on a particular day and, unlike listening to a music playlist you've chosen or watching a Netflix, hayu or Stan series, it's not necessarily curated for you.

- If after looking at other people's posts you start to compare your life with theirs, you can end up feeling like you're not enough. Even though you're smart enough to know that you're comparing yourself to highlights from someone else's life, not their actual life, because of the way our brains work, this still has a negative effect.

Social media is great at connecting us with each other. So my advice is to use it deliberately to do just that – connect. Don't be a voyeur – actually comment on your friends' posts, or DM them to start a real conversation. Liking is passive. Commenting is active, and better. (And do of course remember that seeing your friends IRL is also very important, not to mention great for both your physical and mental health – doing a #DigitalDetox every now and then is the actual best.)

Another hot tip: don't use your social media accounts as your only news source. If you want to keep up with current affairs, check a variety of news sources, whether websites, TV channels, radio stations, podcasts, newspapers or books. If you only consume news on social media, you're more likely to get sucked in by #FakeNews and to get a one-sided view determined by algorithms. For example, if you've ever googled 'Honolulu flights', I bet you noticed that you suddenly started seeing ads from travel companies or airlines promoting flights to Hawaii. This is how digital advertising works. A similar thing happens if you view a lot of news stories about a particular political party – your device will start to serve up more stories about that party. If this is all you're seeing, you can start to think it's the whole picture. Also, the more you engage with an account's posts, the more often they will appear in your feed, crowding out posts from other sources. This is a sure-fire way to become narrow-minded, which in turn risks limiting your career prospects.

When it comes to posting, know that everyone has their own rules about social media – some use it as if they have an audience to entertain, others as if it's their priest or therapist, and others as if it's crazy performance art – and that's a choice everyone gets to make.

But what you publish can have repercussions.

And as we discussed in chapter three, 'How to get noticed', you can play the 'but this is me and the world can deal with it' card as much as you want, but you are responsible for the flow-on effects of how you behave and how you present yourself to the world.

So . . .

IT'S ABOUT BUILDING *real* RELATIONSHIPS

Why publish?

- People choose to work with people they know and like. By having a decent online presence, you're providing a basic introduction to who you are and what you stand for, believe in and like.
- No matter what professional industry you work in, people – including your boss, potential employers and clients – respect good communication skills. Each post you make advertises your skills as a communicator – which can actually be really hard to measure.
- Social media is a great place to talk up your achievements – if something positive has happened to you, it may not be right for your CV but could be perfect for your socials. When the new Wiggles won their first ARIA Award for Best Children's Album, they gave me a shout-out in their acceptance speech. This was such a lovely and unexpected thing for them to do – I think I even teared up a little. Not right for my CV, but the video was perfect for my socials.
- You can promote new projects you're working on – and trust me, clients love it when you get a great story for them on TV, but they also love seeing you promoting their work on your own channels.
- It's FREE marketing. And if you've ever managed budgets before, you'll realise just how valuable this is.

Which platform should I use?

This depends on your target audience and how you can connect with them:

- If your bosses are on LinkedIn and Facebook, perhaps you should be too.
- If your clients are on Instagram, perhaps you should be too.
- If your media contacts are on Twitter, perhaps you should be too.
- If your peers are on Instagram, Snapchat, TikTok, Weibo or WeChat . . . do you get my drift?

Obviously there are only so many hours in the day to be checking, publishing and messaging, and you don't want to live your entire life online – there's a big wide world out there and face-to-face interaction is really important. So you may only concentrate on a couple of these platforms. But having a basic profile on any of the others that your target audience is on will allow you to at least stay in touch and top of mind. Befriend as many people in the industry as you can and make your best posts public.

LinkedIn in particular is becoming more and more important for your career prospects. You need a strong profile that at the very least highlights your education and experience. If you're starting out, I'd also suggest stating what you want in your career and your 'Why'.

What to publish?

Flip back to chapter one, where we talked about what your brand is and what your values are. Read the notes you took.

Then get a refresher on chapter two, where we learnt what your passions are and what your idea of success is, by reviewing the notes you took on this too.

These are good places to start when it comes to deciding what you want to post. Create photos, videos or memes that are in line with your brand and your values:

- Don't publish for 'likes' or even for comments – forget about reaching the masses. Instead, post content that will entertain, educate or engage your audience. It's about reaching the right people and telling the kind of story you want to tell. Don't post anything that's not in line with who you want to be. Trust that content that's genuine and engaging will naturally find its audience. Not all posts become 'leads' that immediately result in something, but one day, one will. And if you post regularly, others will get to know you and you will stay top of mind.
- Posting content that shows you with your workmates, clients or other business contacts shows camaraderie. And people love that – they want in with this great group of people who obviously work well together and share great moments. There's a serious caveat here though: please be mindful of your work's social media policy. You also need to be careful that you're not posting confidential or sensitive information and to be considerate about posting photos of others who may not want them published. If in doubt, check with both that person and your boss. Depending on the industry you work in, you may even need to check with your HR or PR managers. 'Temporary' Insta or Snapchat stories can still cause damage.

- Quality, quality, QUALITY – don't post blurry or pixelated images (unless you're purposely creating art or satire). And don't post photos of your drunken nights out or passive aggressive quotes.
- Keep in mind that your present and potential employers and clients will likely see what you're posting. So think before you do it. As an employer, I've decided that several people who wanted to work with us weren't suitable hires after seeing what they were happy to post on social media, both on their own platforms and in comments on others' posts. Equally, I've hired many people after getting to know them a little better thanks to their social media accounts.

When to publish?

- Consistency is key – ideally you should post once a day or every second day on platforms such as Instagram, Twitter, Snapchat and TikTok if you are managing a business account.
- You can get away with posting a little less frequently on LinkedIn – which makes sense, because a lot of professionals simply don't have the time to be scrolling through social media (and that includes you, so post, browse, comment and connect, then get back to work!). Posts made on weekends tend to receive very low engagement on LinkedIn, so aim for weekdays.
- It's very important to know what's going on in the world before you post. If there's just been a terrible plane crash that's headlining global news, today is not the day to post that pic of you living it up on a flight. If your country is going through an economic crisis, maybe it's not best to post a photo of your expensive new handbag. It's always nice to be sensitive to those around you who may be experiencing heartache.

Is it really worth it?

Yes, yes, a thousand times YES.

Thanks to social media, I've received – and still constantly get – unexpected calls from people wanting to work with us, including:

- a friend of someone I went to school with, because my high school mates see all my posts on Facebook
- a celebrity chef who needed a hand with their social media and who saw my post on Instagram about the amazing meal I had at one of their restaurants
- people who have been referred to us by other publicists who've seen the interesting PR stories I've posted on Twitter and who don't specialise in that area, but can tell that we do and that we really love it
- people who have been referred to us by professionals in other industries who have seen how proudly I talk about our clients on LinkedIn
- our current clients, who want to collaborate with our OTHER clients, because they can see the cool stuff they're up to (and that means more paid work for us!).

The list goes on and on.

Social media also makes my personal life a lot easier. I often get great rates at hotels I regularly stay at thanks to posting on Instagram and Twitter. I don't ever ask for these (frankly, unless you're a serious influencer with a proven, engaged audience that aligns with the hotel's demographic, asking is poor taste), but they're offered, because if I have a genuinely lovely time at a hotel I post about it, and the next time I book they remember me and it's either a reduced rate or a lovely upgrade.

I strike up beautiful new friendships with cafe owners all around the world because I can't stop raving about their excellent flat whites, locally produced salads or smashed avo breakfasts. Then the next time I'm in their city, I get greeted like a long-lost friend and instantly feel like I'm at home (which is downright beautiful when you travel for work as much as I do).

And most importantly, when I've had a crap day, looking back at all the happy and successful posts I've published reminds me that it's not the end of the world and that there are better days ahead.

Quality over quantity

It's not about your number of followers, it's about WHO they are.

If they're your core audience, and they actively engage with you, you're in the best possible situation you can be in.

Don't let massive followings fool you – though if you need mass appeal as part of your end game, then go for it.

But in general, starting small and building genuine followers who are interested in you for the right reasons is the best thing you can do.

And when you know what you're about, and who your target audience is, be careful who you listen to.

Ever read the comments section under a blog or news story? Or a Twitter stream on something controversial?

The majority of the time, these kinds of comments are made by people with no expertise in the field, who have no real interest in you or what you're trying to accomplish.

They're not your target audience. So why listen to them?

#SocialMediaEthics

If you look at my socials, they're mostly bright, fun and beautiful. You're not often going to see pics of me at my desk at 5 am with puffy eyes and no make-up on, or still there at 11 pm with my mascara well and truly smeared, looking like a singer from KISS who's been caught in the rain.

I don't tend to post pics of myself on flights where I'm either on my laptop working the entire time or passed out, attempting to catch up on sleep.

And photos of mouth-watering delicacies tend to get posted over hastily thrown together surprise-in-a-bowl meals made with whatever was still semi-alive in the fridge.

Why? Well, apart from being either too busy or too tired during those moments to take a pic, I'm a visual person and they're not the gorgeous, inspiring photos I want to see when I scroll.

While I do sometimes like to see #RealLife posts from those I follow so that I feel less alone, I know how hard my colleagues and I work, and so do our clients and media partners, so I personally don't need to be constantly reminded of the struggles we faced to get to where we are.

Everyone will have a different view on this. You may find it a refreshing relief to see what's really going on behind the perfectly put together facade of social media. Or you may just want to look at beautiful images as an 'escape' and not be reminded of your own struggles.

Work can be exhausting and draining, especially if you're working with the media or looking after customers online 24/7. Reflecting on achievements and fun times on socials is often the lift I need to keep moving forward. But if anyone looks at our socials and believes that my team and I do nothing but travel, meet celebs and go to parties, remember that this is supported by a lot of hard, very unglam, often tedious behind-the-scenes work. That's what's real.

My 5 simple Insta rules:

1. If the photo you're using isn't yours, always credit and link to the photographer. Also know that some photographers may not want you to use their work at all, so if you're planning to use it commercially, seek approval first.
2. When you're talking about someone else's idea, link to them.
3. Unless you're doing this on purpose for design-related reasons, don't post ten photos in a row from the same event or project – sometimes less is more.
4. Consider whether you need to comment negatively – if you don't like something, could you just not comment at all?
5. Set aside a fixed amount of time for social media each day. Don't waste hours down a rabbit hole.

Come and say hello . . .

Instagram: becbrowncommunications
Twitter: becbrowncomms
LinkedIn: becbrowncommunications
Instagram: thecommsdepartment
Twitter: thecommsdeptHQ
Facebook: thecommsdepartment
Instagram: inkling_design
Instagram: inkling_house

CHAPTER 6

SOUND

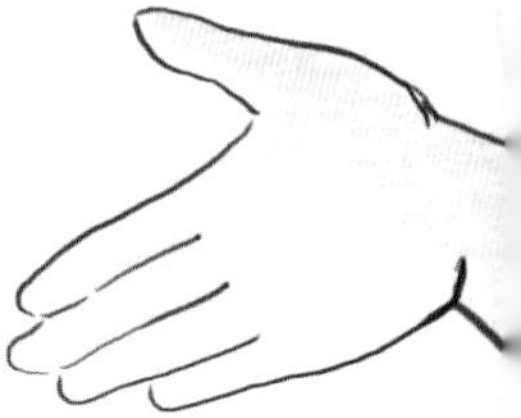

how to speak – the *way* you say something can be as important as *what* you say

Have you ever listened to someone with a really weird or annoying way of speaking and realised that, after they'd finished, you couldn't exactly recall what they said?

This was likely because you'd been so focused on their sound that you didn't take in their words.

This isn't a rare problem and it's something that can happen to any of us if we're not aware of the sound that we're creating. But help is here.

Why is how you sound important?

As I mentioned at the beginning of this book, I started my working life as a singer.

All of those singing lessons, constant hours of practice and the gigs themselves taught me how important it is to listen to yourself as you're performing, and to self-regulate as you go. If a note comes out off-key, you quickly pitch it up or down. If it sounds too shrill, you soften it.

Some of those things can be tricky – you need a good ear to realise what needs to be improved in the first place, and then you need to learn vocal techniques to make the changes required.

How you sound is obviously pretty important when you're belting out a song.

But it's just as important when you're speaking.

It means using your voice purposefully and varying your tone, volume and pace.

The best communicators create an engaging and entertaining experience.

You may have the perfect words to get your point across, but if the person you're trying to convince finds your voice abrasive, monotonous or shrill, they may become defensive, bored or dismissive.

Speaking checklist

The best thing you can do to check what everyone else is hearing is to record yourself speaking. You don't need any special equipment – just use your phone. Play the recording back and pay attention to what you're hearing. Check these five things:

1. Articulation

You don't have to suddenly start speaking like the British royal family, but if you speak clearly with round vowels and clearly define the ends of your words, there won't be any mistaking what you're trying to say.

2. Tone

Is it bright, confident and warm? Dull and dreary? Over-excited and harsh? Listen to it carefully and change it as you need. A great trick that singers use when they want to brighten their tone is to simply smile when they sing. Try this when you speak – your tone instantly becomes warmer and you sound friendlier and more engaging. As we mentioned in chapter four, in the section about conference calls, your tone becomes very important when you're speaking on the phone as there aren't visual cues. Pay close attention to the tone of your voice when you're next on the phone and see how you can play around with it.

3. Pitch

Listen to some of the best speakers – people such as Amanda Keller, Lee Lin Chin or my triple-threat favourite Hugh Jackman. You can also watch TED talks on YouTube, or pick your favourite TV presenter or newsreader (Sandra Sully and Shelly Horton, I'm looking at you). You'll notice that while their pitch varies, they stick to a certain range. Too low and they'd be monotonous and muffled. Too high and they'd be piercing. You want to be easy on the ear so find your ideal range.

Unless you're asking a question, don't go up in pitch at the ends of your words or sentences. This is REALLY IMPORTANT – nothing screams 'I'm an inexperienced junior' like someone who speaks as if their every sentence is a question. If you change nothing else about the way you speak, change this.

4. Volume

Most of us don't have the problem of being too loud – it usually goes the other way, with us speaking too softly. The problem with this is that, not only will people find it hard to hear you, they may also mistake your softness for a lack of confidence. If this is a real issue for you and you struggle to project your voice, it may be worth taking a quick lesson with a vocal or acting coach. Alternatively, jump on YouTube and look for videos that show you how to project your voice. And if presenting, vary your volume from time to time to avoid sounding monotonous.

5. Pace

Take your time as you speak. When you're nervous, it's easy to speak very quickly, which makes it harder for others to understand you. Also, pausing just before or immediately after an important statement adds significant impact to your point. A well-placed pause not only gives you time to think, but also gives your audience a moment to absorb and reflect on your message.

But what if I'm NERVOUS??

'It's okay for you!' I hear you yell. 'You're a trained singer who's used to performing in front of people! When I go to speak in front of loads of people my voice shakes and squeaks and I end up looking and sounding like a hot mess!'

Firstly: great point.

Secondly: no-one, and I mean NO-ONE, is immune to nerves and what they do to your voice.

I've lost count of the number of times I've been in the spotlight at a presentation and felt my palms go sweaty, my breath get shallow and, when I've gone to speak, have almost been unable to recognise the sound that came out.

But it was through these moments that I learnt that I needed to get control of my body back.

So thirdly: **You have options, and they are skills that can be learnt by anyone. So read on . . .**

SPEAKING CHECKLIST

- ☑ articulation
- ☑ tone
- ☑ pitch
- ☑ volume
- ☑ pace

1. Breathe

Calm yourself before you start.

These breathing techniques will calm your body's nervous system and give you a steady platform to speak from.

The following exercise is called **box breathing** and you can do it anywhere – people won't even realise you're doing it:

1. Sitting or standing upright, exhale so all the air is expelled from your body. Then with your mouth closed, take a slow deep breath through your nose, all the way from your tummy, so that your ribs expand outwards as your lungs become full. Do this for a slow count of four.
2. When your lungs are full, hold your breath for another four slow counts.
3. Slowly breathe out again, but this time through your mouth. Do this for a slow count of four.
4. When your lungs are empty, hold your breath for another four counts, and feel your ribs settle back into place.
5. Start the sequence again, breathing in through your nose. Repeat these steps as many times as you need to to feel your breathing deepen and your heart rate slow.

If you're somewhere private, you can do a similar exercise called **alternate nostril breathing**, which can calm you even faster:

1. Place your right hand in front of your nose so that the palm of your hand is facing you.
2. Place your right thumb on the side of your nose so that it blocks your right nostril.
3. Close your mouth and breathe in through your left nostril for a slow count of four. Hold your breath for a second.
4. Place your middle finger over your left nostril, at the same time releasing your thumb from your right nostril, and breathe out through your right nostril for a slow count of four.
5. Breathe in through your right nostril for a slow count of four, then hold your breath for a second.
6. Place your thumb back over your right nostril as you release your middle finger from your left nostril.

7. Repeat these steps, alternating your breathing between each nostril until you're calm.

Note that most people can breathe more easily through one nostril than the other, so if you find one challenging, that's normal. If it's too hard to breathe through one nostril, box breathing may be a better option for you.

2. Visualise

I don't know about you, but if someone sounds awkward and nervous when they're presenting, my heart goes out to them. In the past, I've shuffled in my seat a little, feeling awkward and almost embarrassed for them. These days, I'm more inclined to look at them, smile warmly and nod a little in agreement with what they're saying. They need this visual cue from the room that they're doing okay.

I've done a lot of research and found that, on the whole, humans are really empathetic creatures who wish others well. We can all take heart from this because it means that all the people in the room with us are our personal cheerleaders. They're sitting waiting for us to DO WELL. How cool is that?

This visualising trick always worked for me when I was heading on stage to sing, and easily applies when I need to speak in front of a group.

As you're preparing to speak:

1. Take time to look around the room. Look at people's faces and see them as real, individual humans.
2. Whether you know them or not, imagine that they are close friends or family – people who accept you and love you, flaws and all. Know that it's okay to be vulnerable as you are completely safe.
3. See them as people who have flaws, just like you. And know that if they were to change places with you, they would also be vulnerable, but you would in turn make them feel safe.
4. There is now warmth in the room – these new friends want you to do well. They are interested in what you have to say.
5. Step into this warmth and speak to this beautiful group of friends.

If you're mid-presentation and you feel nerves creep back in, it'll all come down to your breath. It's probably become shallow – you're not taking enough air in and not letting enough out. Slow it down. Pause, take a moment and breathe out. Then breathe in slowly with your ribs expanding again, and start over.

Failing all that, research coming out of Harvard Medical School suggests that when you feel anxiety before any kind of performance that involves speaking, you should try to hijack that fear by telling yourself that it's not anxiety you're feeling – you're actually EXCITED.

Seriously.

The reinterpretation of anxiety as excitement apparently releases different chemicals in your body that stabilise you and actually lead you to become more excited, giving you a mindset focused on opportunity instead of on a perceived threat.

Fascinating, right? Certainly worth a try.

3. Body language

Strike a pose.

Your confidence and ability to articulate what you need to say is increased a thousand times over when you're standing or sitting in a strong way. Not only does your posture influence others, it also influences your brain, and then your voice and actions, to be more powerful.

So sit or stand up straight – make sure you're not slumped.

Uncross your arms, roll your shoulders back, and gently bring your chest up and slightly outwards.

Imagine that there is a vertical string starting from your belly button, going along your backbone, up the back of your neck, out the centre of your skull and up to the ceiling above you, as if a puppeteer is holding you by a single string.

Now gently pull that string upwards and feel yourself rise, one small part of your body at a time.

Feel how it elongates your neck, but keep your chin tucked down a little – don't force your chin to stick out or this will tighten your neck, which restricts both your movement and your voice when you go to speak.

Breathe deeply from way down in your core so that your tummy and ribs expand outwards.

You should feel tall and lean, like a ballerina, but also nimble and free to move around easily.

Speaking shortcuts:

1. Breathe. You've got this.
2. Visualise the warmth coming from those in the room. If you feel any nerves, reframe them as excitement.
3. Check your body language, strike your pose.
4. Pause for a moment so you have time to think about what you'll say and how you'll say it.
5. Concentrate as you speak so that every word you say should be there. Make every word count. If it's unnecessary, don't let it come out of your mouth.
6. Listen to yourself as you speak – how's your articulation, tone, pitch, volume and pace?

Extra tips:

- If you're addressing a group, forget about thinking that you have to 'speak to the masses' and really focus on speaking to just one person.
- Be yourself. But be an upbeat version of it. People want to be inspired, entertained or informed (and they won't be if you look like you've swallowed a bottle of valium!).
- You're the one in control. Did I mention that you've got this?

CHAPTER 7

MANAGING YOU

building your work into an extraordinary life (minus the burnout)

Picture this.

You've scored an incredible job in the industry of your dreams.

Excitement levels are high – this is what you've worked so hard for.

But now that you're here, working hard feels like the ONLY thing you do.

Days start early and finish late, the deadlines are relentless, your boss continues to pile work on you, and you have to report to multiple people whose priorities all seem to conflict.

So even though the work itself is thrilling, there's just too much of it.

While the idea of running your career at full pace 24/7 may seem like the way to get ahead, the only thing that I can guarantee is that you won't be able to keep this up.

Short bursts of hard work and long hours are reasonable. A never-ending marathon is not.

After taking the marathon approach and nearly burning out (more on this in chapter twelve), my aim became to create a sustainable career.

I want my personal and professional lives to improve over time, and not end in a crashing heap.

If this is the approach you'd like to take too, well done on a wise move.

So how do you do this?

This simple concept is a good start:

> Cultivate two things equally – structure and flexibility.
>
> They're going to be your two best friends.
>
> And they go together like yin and yang, salt and caramel, air and breathing, and Chrissy Teigen and John Legend.
>
> They may be different but they're complementary, and combined they create something extraordinary.

Structure is the routines and boundaries you put in place that allow you to manage both your professional and personal lives. It carves out blocks of time and creates a safe space for you to work and play in.

Flexibility is how you can adapt within that structure as demands are placed on you.

Put simply, I couldn't do the job that I do, or run the business that I have, without both of these things in equal measure.

The best PR and communications professionals are very organised. They map out strategic results-driven plans and have procedures in place to ensure there's consistency in their work and that deadlines are being met.

But life throws surprises at us, and working in a media environment that is 'always on' means there are days when we need to respond to a situation immediately, throwing our schedule straight out the window. We have to pivot and adapt. So we re-prioritise on the spot and move less important things to another day (communicating with those who need to know) so that we can concentrate on what's unfolding.

French novelist Gustave Flaubert embraced this idea too, when he said, 'Be regular and orderly in your life, so that you may be fierce and original in your work.'

It took me a while to make this combo work for me, as I didn't particularly like structure. I found it constricting and boring. But without it, I bounced around all over the place and never really got anything done. My mental and physical health fluctuated a lot as I didn't have very consistent eating, exercise or sleep habits.

But too much structure *can* be limiting. You miss out on great opportunities because you're too fixed on your plans – so this is where flexibility comes into play.

In spite of working in a very chaotic and fast-paced creative industry full of events, unpredictable media requests and long, often unconventional hours, I focus on having a healthy and relatively structured lifestyle.

This means using a yearly calendar, with plans loosely mapped out twelve months in advance, and the next two months planned out in much more detail.

Every week I create a to-do list, and every night, before I shut down my computer, I map out my next day.

I include everything in my to-do list and calendar – from work to exercise, to personal appointments, to catch-ups with friends and family.

But I do, where possible, leave buffer time for unpredictable things, so that when these occur I can be flexible and move things around.

You can apply this approach to the table you created as part of chapter two, where you sorted your goals into five categories: work, personal, family & friends, health, and financial.

This means that when you structure your time, it needs to be divided five ways.

If you're working full time (or currently studying with the goal of working full time), you'll realise that you need to be strategic to ensure you have enough time for the other four categories.

Can you map out activities for one month across these five categories?

From there, you can start your daily to-do list, but try not to overload it.

What's mandatory and what's less important that could be shifted to tomorrow or the end of the week?

Have you allowed extra time for all the unexpected things you will need to deal with?

At the end of the week, and again at the end of the month, assess how you've gone. Sometimes it's much better to look at what you've achieved over the course of a month, rather than a day or week. While you might feel you've had an unproductive day from time to time, you can still have a productive month.

Work–life balance versus career–life flow

I'm not a fan of the phrase 'work–life balance'.

> It makes me think of a playground seesaw – put too much weight on one side (work) and the other side shoots up, empty (life). So we try and balance things out by putting more weight on the empty side.

> But then all we seem to do is keep adding more weight to both sides, in an endless struggle to even things up. We end up overloading the seesaw so that both sides are so heavy it feels as if our whole life might just snap in half and shatter.

It's also a bit of a weird phrase because there isn't actually a 'work life' and a 'real life' – it's all just life. But for the sake of making things easy to visualise and explain, I personally aim to have what I call **'career–life flow'**.

This goes back to the idea of being flexible and is about how you integrate your career into other parts of your life.

> **Your career is your actual day-to-day job, plus the planning, admin and relationships with colleagues, business partners and other stakeholders it involves.**
>
> **Your life is your family, friends, downtime, hobbies, life admin, fitness and sleep. (And there may be some overlap between your life and career – I'm sure that, as is the case for me, many of your work colleagues or clients are also great friends of yours.)**
>
> **Your flow is how you move between all these activities and people.**

I firmly believe that in the future businesses will reward those who can best manage their career–life flow.

Because we simply no longer live in a world where you clock in at nine on Monday and out at five on Friday and have weekends off.

And those of us in creative industries have probably never worked with this kind of structure! Musicians mostly rehearse during the day and work in the afternoons, at night and on weekends. Many artists work at the times of the day that best suit their creativity.

And no matter what industry we're in, we're contactable all the time and have the ability to work globally thanks to technology, which means all hours of the day are open to us.

But we shouldn't be working all of them. As humans, we're not wired to be able to do that.

We need time out of work to spend with our loved ones, to concentrate on other passions, and to rest and recharge.

This is where career–life flow comes into play.

The old-school arrangement of working for eight hours and then ignoring work completely when you're not at your workplace is outdated in many industries.

Instead, you might have the option of splitting your day into smaller blocks of time for different career and life activities. There may be some days where you switch activities every three or four hours, and other days that are divided into even shorter blocks.

For example, if you work a traditional Monday to Friday job, your day could potentially look like this:

6–8 am – 2 hours of personal time – exercising, eating breakfast and getting ready at home

8–9 am – 30 minutes of personal time plus 30 minutes of work time – catching up on social media and work emails on your commute

9 am–12 pm – 3 hours of work at your workplace

12–1 pm – 1 hour of personal time – having lunch, maybe seeing a friend, plus a small amount of social media or online browsing time

1–5.30 pm – 4.5 hours of work at your workplace

5.30–7.30 pm – 2 hours of personal time – socialising, eating dinner, or life admin

7.30–8 pm – 30 minutes of work emails

8–10 pm – 2 hours of personal time – socialising, relaxing, or life admin, then winding down. Try not to use screens (laptops, TV or phones) in the hour before you go to sleep.

That's given you just over eight hours of work time and almost eight hours of personal time in one day. You're checking into work often enough to hopefully keep everyone there happy, and the blocks of time are long enough to ensure that your attention isn't scattered, which means you don't feel as if you're leaping from project to project every five minutes. Perfect. (Though do know that there will always be exceptions to this eight-hour work day if you are building a business or working on an important time-sensitive project. Often there will be times when you need to work for longer periods and this will leave less time for other activities. But to avoid burnout, this needs to be balanced out by scheduling more personal downtime.)

If you work part time while studying, start early or finish late, or have multiple jobs, the same rules apply. You flow calmly through one activity, then decide to end it for the moment. You acknowledge that it's done and that you're now moving on to something else, and so the flow continues.

While flowing gives you flexibility (and sounds quite relaxing!), it still requires structure and discipline.

You need to be firm in setting boundaries so that you allow enough time to focus on your career activities and enough time to focus on your life activities.

Flow does NOT mean multitasking. It means consciously starting one activity, finishing it, pausing for a moment, then beginning the next.

Multitasking has also been shown to be a fallacy. Multiple studies by doctors and neuroscientists have revealed that the brain cannot multitask. When you're seemingly doing several things at once, you're actually just moving incredibly quickly between one task and the next. And if you're doing this a lot over an extended period of time, your brain becomes exhausted and you're usually not doing a particularly good job of anything.

Which is why old-school multitasking can be one of the fastest ways to burn out.

So slow it down.

Choose one task and move through it. Choose to stop that first task and move on to the next. And repeat.

It's ebb and flow.

You will have to decide what the most important thing to be focusing on is. Where are you most needed right now?

This becomes empowering because you are the one making the decision.

Even if you're doing a certain task because your boss has told you it's a priority, you're still the one choosing to be in this job.

Powerful, right?

So if I'm working on a big project with a tight deadline, I will choose to work sixteen-hour days for five days in a row to get it done.

But when it's done, I choose to rest and recover, focusing on the things I love – usually sleep, family and fitness.

It's crucial to note that structuring your day should not involve breaking up your sleep at night. Sleep is critical and studies show that 98 per cent of humans need a minimum of 8–9 hours of sleep per night. Too many of us think we're in the 2 per cent that need less, but this is very unlikely. (New parents looking after little ones are the exception here, but that's when napping becomes important!)

What to do when you can't switch off

Even if you are passionate about your job and feel you have the energy of a thousand entrepreneurs, do you sometimes feel that work occupies too much of your life?

Or more simply, do you often feel like you can't switch off?

Here's how to manage that in two easy steps.

1. Get the data

While *doing* your actual job no doubt takes up a lot of time, how much time do you spend *thinking* (or stressing) about work?

This doesn't mean the sort of thinking that problem-solving entails, as that's technically doing the work.

But how much time do you spend unproductively thinking, stressing or worrying about anything to do with your job?

Let's work it out.

Grab your notebook and map out a week, Monday to Sunday.

Write down the windows of time outside of your normal work hours where you're thinking about work or your career – ruminating without actually solving anything. Does this happen when you're in the shower, when you're eating breakfast, when you're commuting to work, during your lunch break, when you're commuting home from work, when you're at the gym, when you're eating dinner, when you're half on social media/half watching TV, or when you're trying to go to sleep?

If you can't estimate the amount of time you spend unproductively thinking about work, track this in your diary for a week.

It's time to reclaim that time.

2. Create boundaries – both physical and mental

- Over the next week, try to **set times that you will devote to work, and others that you won't**. If you work a lot, be generous with these times in the first instance. Let's say you're going to allow work time to be 8 am–7 pm from Monday to Friday, 10 am–12 pm on Saturday or 5 pm–6 pm on Sunday (work out blocks that suit you best). If you find yourself thinking about work *at all* outside of these times, gently remind yourself that those thoughts are out of bounds, and shift your focus back to whatever else you were doing.

- To follow up on the previous point, **always have a cut-off time for work each night**. I start work really early and work in an 'always on' environment so my hours are probably more extended than some, but unless it's an emergency or I'm working to a deadline or I'm at an event, my absolute cut-off is 8 pm. Often I finish earlier than that, but at least I have a cut-off. That means no emails, checking socials or work calls or texts. This gives me plenty of time to wind down so that I can get a good night's sleep.
- When you get home and your work time has ended, **change the mood**. Alter the lighting to make it softer, put your favourite music on, or light some candles. Over time, these physical cues will help you to shift from work mode to relax or play mode.
- If you're working when you're at home, **have one set working space**. Don't allow work to encroach on every part of your home, or you'll feel like you can never escape it. Your workspace might be the dining room table, your desk, or a particular chair in your lounge room. Choose one spot where work gets done. Everywhere else is out of bounds (especially your bedroom. Your bed should be a place for sleep or fun . . . and that's it!).
- Again, if you are working from home, **allocate certain clothes as 'work clothes'**. And once you've finished your work, change out of them. This outfit change prompts your body and mind to shift modes.
- If social media is work-related for you and being on it makes you think about work in any way, then **switch off your socials at your set time**. For me, that's usually 8 pm on weeknights and varies on weekends, depending on what other activities I have planned.
- This should go without saying, but **when you're at work, WORK**. Ten minutes here or there on social media or doing online shopping or other mindless activities doesn't make your workday shorter, it makes it longer! All those wasted minutes mean that some of your work now needs to be done out of hours, which eats into the rest of your life.

How to speak with your boss or client when you're struggling

If you've assessed how you're spending your time, created structures and boundaries that you've put into practice for at least a month (while still remaining flexible to life's ebb and flows), worked to your strengths where you can and taken care of yourself by maintaining good sleep, diet, exercise and social habits, and are STILL struggling, it's time to look more closely at what's going on at work.

Perhaps your boss *is* putting unreasonable demands on your time. Maybe your clients *do* have unrealistic expectations.

> This is when you need to put your communications superpowers to work and speak up.

Before you do this, know that it's normal to think, 'They're going to think I'm incompetent, that I can't handle my work, that I'm being difficult, that I'm lazy. Maybe it's just easier to go along with it so that I don't get fired.'

But if you don't speak up, the greater risk is that you will burn out, which is likely going to have far worse consequences.

These pointers will help you to counter that. And in fact this approach can be used any time you have a disagreement:

- **Don't anticipate the worst.** Yes, your boss or client may be surprised or annoyed when you go to them, but if you do this the right way and at the right time, it's unlikely to affect your career progression (and if it does, well, if your boss or client is that unreasonable, with all due respect to them, you may politely want to exit stage left on that gig anyway).
- **Find the right time.** If you feel the conversation is worth the risk, find the best time for it. If you're in the middle of a huge project the whole team is working around the clock to complete, consider waiting until it's done so that your boss or client is in the right headspace. If you can, check their calendar for both work and personal events to find out when is a good time to speak with them.
- **Find the right approach.** Face-to-face conversations generally produce the best results as tone and visual cues can be taken into account, which often takes the heat out of a challenging situation. But there are always exceptions to rules. How does your boss or client like to receive information? Are they predominantly verbal or written communicators? In the next chapter we'll cover the

differences between introverts and extroverts. Consider which one you think they are. Does this change your understanding of the way they might like to receive this kind of feedback?

- **Stay calm.** If you're getting flustered, quietly use the box breathing technique you learnt in chapter six (page 83). The more calmly you approach this, the calmer the other person will be too.
- **What do you both value?** Chances are, the reason you're being worked so hard is that your boss or client wants the best result for their company. But what exactly is this? Can you pinpoint it? Is it making more sales, increasing profits, getting a project done on time, or simply looking good to *their* boss? When you talk to your boss or client about needing to reduce your workload, make it clear to them that their concern is one that you share and that it's important to you as well. This empathy will show them that you're not just thinking about yourself but appreciate their needs too.
- **Be clear.** Calmly articulate the problem. Explain what the issue is, how you've already tried to counter it and how long you've tried this for. Demonstrate that you understand the shared goal you're both working towards and have been prioritising it, but explain that it's now becoming unsustainable and that you're concerned that, if things remain the way they are, either mistakes will be made or you won't be able to continue.
- **Avoid the blame game.** Try your best to not use judgemental language that puts your boss or client personally at fault. They have likely been working really hard on the project too, and managing people or suppliers is just one part of their job. If you tell them they've been unreasonable or unrealistic, all they'll hear is that they don't know how to do their job or that they're doing it badly. Remember that, even if they look like they have it all together, they're people too, and no-one likes to be criticised. So present facts instead of judgement. Instead of saying, 'You're expecting me to do the work of two people and that's not fair and doesn't make sense,' try, 'Since Alicia left the company three months ago, she hasn't been replaced and I've been allocated all of her work in addition to my own. While I've tried to manage this for as long as I can, it's now become unsustainable.'
- **Humbly offer a solution.** If you have one, suggest it, but do so graciously. If you don't have a solution, make it clear that if they're

happy for you to assist them, you're willing to work with them to find one as soon as possible. Or if it's up to them to work out a solution, thank them for their time and energy and also remind them that they've got this. Sometimes those higher up than you need encouragement too.

Essential four-step life management checklist:

1. **Sleep.** If you change nothing else about your lifestyle, for the love of everything you cherish, get good sleep! It's crucial for memory, concentration, creativity, productivity, immunity, weight control, stress management, longevity and more. Everyone is different but chances are you need somewhere between 8 and 9 hours of sleep a night at a minimum. If you can't nail this, is there any way you can take a short nap during the day? Back when I worked at Universal Music, I managed PR for a very hardworking and successful celebrity artist from Europe. His management team made me block out an hour of his publicity schedule every afternoon so he could have a quick siesta at 2.30 pm. After he left the country, inspired by his boundless energy, on days that I could manage it I'd go to my car in the afternoon, set my phone timer to twenty minutes, lock the doors and have a power nap. If I wasn't tired, I'd still go to my car and meditate. This gave me an instant energy boost that lasted the rest of the afternoon and into the night and I was soon hooked. Twenty minutes is the perfect amount of time as you wake refreshed and haven't been asleep long enough to feel groggy.
2. **Nutrition and exercise.** When life gets hectic, these are often the first things that get neglected. But it's actually during stressful times that you need them most. I'm not a dietician or nutritionist so I won't give detailed advice, but what I do know is that everyone has an eating style that works best for their body, and all the research seems to agree that eating when you're hungry, eating a combination of high-quality carbs, lean protein and good fats, and drinking eight or more glasses of water a day is the way to go. Stick to whole foods, eat your vegetables, and minimise sugar, caffeine and alcohol. As for exercise, wow, what a powerful

and happy punch of energy that can give us! When you exercise, your body produces feel-good chemicals such as endorphins, endocannabinoids and oxytocin. These make your brain more resilient to stress, increase your motivation, and make you more optimistic, hopeful and sociable. There are many studies that have proven this, and for more information, check out **Kelly McGonigal's** book, ***The Joy of Movement: How exercise helps us find happiness, hope, connection, and courage***, which I discuss in chapter sixteen. So if you're having one of those days where you just don't want to be around people, going for a run, dancing or taking a HIIT class will actually empower you to connect and share more with others. It's like having a chemist in your body that releases happy drugs every time you get your heart rate up or contract your muscles. Incredible, huh?

3. **Community.** All of the science proves that humans are wired for connection and that, without it, we falter, both physically and mentally. So every day, try to spend time IRL with your friends and family, whether this involves going for a 30-minute walk or having a meal or a cup of tea. And give and receive a hug – that physical connection releases endorphins and oxytocin (cutely named 'the cuddle hormone' by scientists) into your body that will nourish and soothe you. If you can't do these things, get on the phone and video-call someone instead, so you can see each other's faces. Failing that, just voice-call so you can at least hear one another. Texting and messaging are optional add-ons – they simply cannot replace time spent in person or looking at another human's face.

4. **Work to your strengths.** When it comes to productivity, all times of the day are not equal. We all have an in-built body clock that regulates our circadian rhythms and controls when we feel awake and tired over a 24-hour period. We each have a different chronotype, which basically determines whether we're a morning person (a lark), a night person (an owl), or somewhere in between. Knowing where you fall on this spectrum will help you determine when you should try to perform different tasks. The best time to work out which chronotype you have is when you're on holidays and have a week or so to go to bed when

you're naturally tired and to wake up without an alarm clock. Failing that, take note of when you naturally go to sleep and wake up on a quiet weekend. Larks and in-between birds do their best work in the morning, whereas owls work best in the late afternoon or evening. Where possible, larks and in-between birds should try to do any analytical tasks or decision-making in the morning, and save their afternoons for more routine work such as admin and answering easy emails. Owls would reverse this approach and try to do easier work in the morning and more analytical tasks in the afternoon or early evening. While the traditional work day is more suited to larks and in-betweeners, owls can still try to tweak their tasks and schedules to suit their strengths. For more information on this topic, I'd highly recommend reading **Daniel Pink's** book ***When: The scientific secrets of perfect timing***. In addition to your circadian rhythm, you may want to optimise your output by working with your infradian rhythm. What's that, I hear you ask? Super simple – this is your menstrual cycle. Chances are you'll have more energy in the first two thirds of your cycle, and a little less in the final third. With this in mind, can you load up activities that are within your control in the first part of your cycle and schedule less towards the end?

Know that managing your life – both professionally and personally – is a project you'll always be working on. Some weeks you'll have it all together and feel as if you're expertly and gracefully spinning plates with the ease of a seasoned circus pro. Other weeks you'll feel as if you'll never get everything done and – to use an excellent phrase that my colleague Tina recently introduced me to – it's as if you're unsuccessfully trying to juggle jelly.

But as you learn and try out new techniques, and as you become better at prioritising what's truly important and letting go of the things that aren't, you should feel confident that you're becoming a wonderful manager of your own life.

And if you face any challenges along the way, well, that's just what comes with having a full, exciting and meaningful life. And that sure beats the alternative, right?

TOGETHER,
STRUCTURE & FLEXIBILITY
CREATE SOMETHING
extraordinary

CHAPTER 8

INTROVERTS & EXTROVERTS

learn which one you are and
then use this to your advantage

Do you feel that you're an introvert or an extrovert?

How about those you work with?

What's the difference?

Why is this even important?

Discovering the answers to these four questions can be one of those lightbulb moments that suddenly make everything click into place.

There are varying theories about what makes an introvert or an extrovert. You can take personality tests that will define you as one or the other but it's actually not that simple.

While there are many shades of grey in this area, most theories seem to agree that introversion and extroversion aren't entirely about whether you're quiet and shy, or loud and confident (as most people think); they're also about **where you get your energy from**.

> Introverts need solitude to recharge their batteries, while extroverts draw their energy from others.

It's important to know this so that you can better work to your strengths.

You can also work better with other people once you know what energises and lifts them.

The world's population is apparently split roughly fifty-fifty into introverts and extroverts. And the majority of people fall somewhere between extreme introversion and extreme extroversion.

Introverts may:

- do their best work alone
- have a strong ability to concentrate when left alone
- prefer to text or email rather than call
- prefer to have a limited number of friends
- feel that spending the entire evening socialising with a large group of people or being in a noisy environment drains their battery
- be described as calm and deliberate
- consider the perfect Friday night being at home with family, close friends or even alone.

The stereotype is that introverts are often shy and timid and don't make good leaders. That's actually not true – while they may be sensitive to their surroundings, they're also really alert and responsive as well.

Extroverts may:

- do their best thinking out loud, often with an audience
- be known for their speaking and networking skills
- feel comfortable communicating under pressure
- present their ideas more forcefully
- be described as the life of the party
- feel energised where there's a buzz around them – when they're listening to music or the radio or just the noise of people chattering nearby
- love big events with lots of people, such as sporting events, parties and festivals.

The stereotype is that extroverts need to be the centre of attention and aren't good at listening or paying attention to detail. That's not necessarily true either – they just feel energised by being around others, which means they're well suited to networking and working with big teams of people.

So which of these descriptions is ringing true for you?

Most people will be able to work out whether they're an introvert or extrovert simply reading the lists above. And a heads up that if you google 'introvert extrovert test' and start taking various personality quizzes online, it gets a bit more complex. This is because of the different theories out there and the shades of grey on the introvert–extrovert spectrum – some introverts who recharge through solitude are shy and quiet while others are more confident and outspoken, and some extroverts who derive their energy from others are lively and loud while others have milder mannerisms.

Essentially, there's no 'one size fits all' label, as we're all a blend of characteristics. So if you take different online tests, you may end up with varying results, but you should start to skew one way or the other.

Personally, on the basis of where I get my energy from, I'm much more of an introvert.

This shocked me when I first realised it. I was in my late twenties and a friend who was studying psychology explained the theories to me. I'd figured that because I'd worked on stage and screen as a performer and am very happy in front of an audience, a packed boardroom or a camera – and because I'm quick to respond to people and will usually be the first one to greet everyone in the room – I was an extrovert.

> But I'll say this again as it's worth repeating: it's also about where you get your energy from.

Being around people all the time exhausts me. More than two coffees a day and I'm a jittery mess. Loud music and constant chatter don't amp me up, they make me want to hide under my desk.

While I love a busy day full of meetings, working on and attending huge events, and going to music concerts, I need to break these things up with a lot of quiet time, which means I then naturally gravitate towards interactions that are one-on-one or with a small group of people.

Introverts are easily stimulated. Things may affect them more – noise, energetic people, bright lights and maybe even caffeine, sugar and scents, for example.

The upside to this is that when you're 'on', you're SO ON! The downside is that without carefully monitoring your energy stores, you suddenly flip and can feel really overwhelmed and even burnt out.

You'd think this would make me a terrible PR, but it's quite the opposite. I'm strategic about how I spend my time. And because I factor in downtime, I can do my planning in a calm and measured way.

To recharge, I spend a lot of time alone or with a couple of close friends who know me so well that I don't need to be 'on'. I'm very happy in my own company, spending time reading, running, swimming or doing yoga.

Here are the huge career-building positives to being an introvert:

It can make you **a great listener** – you don't need to be the centre of attention or the one always talking. This allows you to be more receptive and gives you space to come up with creative ideas. Knowing how to assess a situation carefully and to think before you speak allows you to present a clear and succinct message. This is a valuable skill and something I train our clients who are spokespeople for their businesses to do too.

If you're fine with spending time by yourself, you likely also have a **strong ability to concentrate when left alone**. When you're starting a business and there are millions of hours of work to do, this is possibly the most useful skill ever.

This can also **make solving complex problems easier** – spending time researching, analysing and problem-solving can be fun to an introvert because you get to sit there and delve into the work without distractions from other people.

Being an introvert has made me **a good writer**. Because I can sit alone and think about things very carefully, I can work through a challenging concept and turn it into something succinct and palatable.

Introverts are also **observers**. When you're not busy being a doer, you can take the time to observe and, as a result, get the full picture much more easily. Your eagle eyes can pick up things that others miss – from what's said (or not said) to how others' relationships work (or don't work) – and acting on these observations can lead to incredible business opportunities.

> One of the reasons I've deliberately outlined the strengths of introversion is that, historically, a lot of introverts have had a tougher time in traditional working environments. Many introverts have been told that they're too sensitive, quiet, reserved, boring, or not team players. And if this is something you're concerned about or have already experienced, I want you to feel reassured that you're not alone and that you can make your introvert superpowers work for you.

Discovering the pros of introversion also made me feel a lot better about myself. Previously I'd often feel confused about how I could be so confident and friendly on some days and feel like completely avoiding the world on other days. These shifts in attitude made me feel a bit crazy, as if I was made up of two conflicting personalities and ultimately wasn't handling life very well. But once I discovered the introvert–extrovert spectrum, I was able to better understand myself. I also started to become more curious about others and how I could better relate to them.

So that's me as an introvert. But you should also **meet my brilliant and successful friend, Tom, who's an extrovert**.

Tom has a big personality – he's busy, loud, a big-picture thinker, and full of incredible, BOLD ideas.

He is fabulous – people flock to him because he's fun and has great energy. You never know what he's going to come up with next, which is highly entertaining. He's one of those charismatic, inspiring people you just want to be around (and he loves this because he's even more fabulous when he has an audience!).

And his access to lots of inspiring people has led to great business opportunities.

He's also excellent at thinking on his feet and verbalising his ideas quickly, which means he's often able to convince others that his ideas are the smartest thing they've ever heard.

But here are the challenges Tom faces, as he explained to me:

- He's not good at stillness or being alone, so he struggles with details and follow-through in both his professional and personal lives because he finds it hard to spend the necessary hours at his computer creating the plan.
- He's often so boldly ON that he misses subtle cues around him (and may not be aware when he has accidentally offended someone).
- He's terrible at rolling out a plan with a high level of attention to detail because he's so easily distracted by exciting things going on around him. You'd think this could be easily fixed by teaming him up with a detail-oriented 'doer' – but . . .
- Others are sometimes reluctant to work with him because, despite his obvious charisma, he can come off as scatty, hard to pin down and, occasionally, very abrasive.

So given these challenges, why is Tom so successful?

Because he combines his strengths with strategic sacrifices, sometimes forgoing his need for noise and drama in favour of silent study.

And because he knows that the end result – an incredibly successful project – trumps his needs as an extrovert.

He also knows that he should ideally try to work with others who are happy to be around his intense energy but who are also detail-oriented enough to carry out his big plans; or he'll sometimes deliberately tone down that intense energy to ensure he doesn't put everyone offside.

My colleagues, clients, media contacts and other business partners are a mix of introverts and extroverts, which is fantastic because, between us, we have all bases covered.

And really importantly, by knowing everyone's personality type, I can help them work to their strengths.

> This awareness of others will become one of your communication superpowers.
>
> Once you know who's an introvert and who's an extrovert, you can tailor the way you communicate with them so that your message is received in the best possible way.

As a general rule, many introverts absorb information better in written form – in email or text, for example.

Meanwhile, many extroverts prefer to have a verbal conversation.

There's no hard-and-fast rule and you'll need to experiment to know what your preferences are. Everyone is different, so you'll need to talk to others to find out what works best for them.

As an introvert, if I'm faced with a challenging situation and have to give someone critical feedback, I'd personally rather write it all down, because I can articulate my thoughts more clearly in writing. I may still deliver that news verbally, but I'll write it down first to consolidate it. And I'd often rather read critical feedback than have it delivered in person, so that I can take it in, process it and decide what to do about it.

But I also know that many extroverts don't always like giving or receiving news in writing. So if I have an extroverted client or colleague and need to receive or deliver news – whether good or bad – chances are it will be smarter for me to pick up the phone or to go and see them in person. Do I always want to do that? No. Do I always have time to do that? No. But do I know that it's going to result in a better outcome? Hell yes. So wherever possible, that's what I try to do.

WHERE DO YOU GET YOUR *energy* FROM?

And the great thing is that, over time, you become much better at recognising other people's traits and it becomes easier and easier to adapt your communication style to suit them.

> **Warning: Don't let the label 'introvert' or 'extrovert' define who you are.**
>
> **You are a multidimensional human being and lots of other factors will influence how you live your life.**

Extroverts – this isn't your chance to say, 'Well, I'm just naturally loud and outgoing and the life of the party, so everyone had better get used to it!'

Introverts – I'd better not hear you say, 'Well, sorry boss, I can't go to that meeting because all those people will drain my energy, so I'm heading home now to get my energy back.'

While it's good to know your personality traits, what you choose to *do* is also extremely important.

While I may be an introvert in that I need time away from others to recharge my batteries, there are other parts of my life – such as my sense of purpose and my passions – that also greatly affect my wellbeing, and the pursuit of these things sometimes requires me to 'act out of character'.

For example, after a long week, I might not want to go to a big party with lots of loud people and even louder music. However, I know that my going there – to celebrate a friend's birthday or to network, which will benefit my clients – will have a greater positive effect on my wellbeing, and therefore I go. In that way *acting* as an extrovert trumps my need to *be* an introvert because I have that higher purpose.

I'll say this again, because it's important:

> **Knowing if you are an introvert or extrovert is really helpful, but what you do matters more.**

So if you're working towards a goal, don't let your introversion or extroversion get in your way. Use the parts of your personality you can to your advantage, and step over other parts if you need to. If your goal is important to you, I promise you'll be strong enough to achieve it.

CHAPTER 9

MANAGING UP

best ways to work with
your boss, get a promotion
and deal with office politics

Knowing how to manage other people is a learnt skill.

But so is managing your boss or others above you – it's called 'managing up', and when you're rising through the ranks, being able to do this well is a game changer.

Let me tell you what managing up *isn't*.

It's not:

- sucking up
- kissing ass
- flattering
- manipulating.

> It is seeking out powerful people to:
>
> - assist them to do great work
> - learn from them.
>
> When you do these things consistently, you'll cultivate favour.
>
> Doing these two things is also a huge demonstration of leadership potential. And that's what we call a win-win situation.

American author Ryan Holiday has a great book called *Ego Is the Enemy*. He's also done a bunch of media and podcast interviews about this idea. Among many other helpful life lessons, he talks about 'being a canvas for other people's work'.

This is very different to being a doormat – allowing others to take credit for your work or to step all over you on their way to the top. It's about simultaneously being a shadow, a doer and a sponge – observing, getting the job done as directed by the expert, and taking in all the information flowing in that moment so that you can learn from it.

To quote Ryan: 'It's not about making someone *look* good. It's about providing the support so that others can *be* good . . . Clear the path for the people above you and you will eventually create a path for yourself.'

Chances are you'll feel like some of the work you are asked to do is beneath you. You may feel it's too basic – after all, you may even have tertiary qualifications in your field!

But put this aside for a while.

Apart from the simple fact that for the company to run (and therefore give you the job that you have) someone has to do these things, this is the time for on-the-job training. And when you leave your ego at the door, even if it's shouting 'you're entitled to more!', you'll find that this is the fastest way to arrive at that point in your career where you have earned a higher title (and salary to match).

So we've covered the concept of learning from those above you while assisting them to do great work. But what are some other strategies that you can use to access their valuable time and attention? These all relate to a trait that's thankfully becoming more prevalent in today's work environment – and that's empathy.

> **Empathy is the ability to understand and share the feelings of someone else. It's the foundation of great relationships and can help to build teams and communities.**
>
> **It's also a great way to uncover what drives your boss or any of the senior executives who are in your sights.**

How can you get to know these people better?

Are they on LinkedIn or other social media platforms they'd be happy to connect with you on? If so, re-read chapter five, 'Social media: Dos and don'ts', for some pointers. And look at what they are publishing – what's important to them? Chances are they're really invested in the commercial success of the company and, aside from reading your company's annual report or similar material, a great way to learn more about what may be impacting this success is to look at trade media publications relevant to your industry. In the PR and comms industry in Australia, for example, this includes media publications and websites such as *AdNews*, *B&T*, *Mediaweek*, *Mi3* and *Mumbrella*, and the business, media or communications sections of newspapers such as the *Australian Financial Review*, the *Australian*, the *Sydney Morning Herald*, the *Age* and the *Guardian*. If there are stories that are interesting to you, share them on your socials. And if there are positive stories published about your company, share those with pride too – your bosses will be impressed by the support you're showing your company.

You can of course also just ask questions of those you work with – your colleagues and your boss's assistant can be great sources of information. So if you don't already know them well, find a time when they're not busy and begin cultivating a relationship with them.

Alternatively, is there an opportunity for you to volunteer to be more involved with the communications or culture departments within your company? Could you assist with social media or internal communications? Does your company have a social team that organises events or works with charities? If so, could you volunteer your time there? These are spaces where relationships are built, and, just like empathy, good communication leads to better teams and communities, all things that are likely to be valuable to your bosses.

How to nail your performance review and stay on track for a promotion

Most organisations will have formal performance reviews. Often they're done annually, though many excellent companies hold them more regularly – for example, quarterly (The Comms Department included).

These reviews are usually designed so that you can give and receive feedback with your manager on how you're performing in your role. They're also the time to ask about promotions and salary increases.

Here's how to prepare:

- **What's the deal?** Different companies have varying procedures for reviews so, when you get your job, ask how they work – when are they, who are they with, if there is an agenda, if there is work that needs to be completed before the day, if it is casual or a presentation, and if this is when promotions and raises are assessed. Closer to the date, read the company manual or ask HR or your manager for more details. Talk to your co-workers who have been with the business for a while too, as many of them will be able to give you the inside goss on what to expect.
- **Prepare.** Make a list of all that you've accomplished for the company. Pull out significant moments and clearly explain how those achievements have benefited the company. If you have evidence of this in the form of positive emails from customers or other stakeholders, include these too. Know that on the day you may hear some criticism. This is normal, so be ready for it and be willing to accept it. A good manager will ensure that it's not personal but professional, so don't see this as an attack, because it's not. If, after listening carefully to it

and asking questions for clarity, you disagree, say so and explain why. But do this very calmly – this is not the time to become defensive. If your manager's style is a little outdated or they're simply not good at these kinds of things (which is often the way), be prepared for that too. Not everyone is a good communicator so cut them some slack.

- **Make it about them.** While this is your review, you only have this job because the company has been successful enough to give it to you. So make your review about the company too. Ask about the business's development – how is it tracking and where is it going? By showing interest in the company, you're demonstrating that you're thinking of the bigger picture and not only your role. And ask how you can help with these business goals. Doing these things shows that you have the traits of a good manager. Listen carefully to their answers as what's being relayed may impact how you steer the rest of your conversation or presentation. Ask your manager how they're going too. This shows your empathy and willingness to understand the business's demands on them and others like them. It also shows that you're a nice human!
- **Be your own PR.** It's time to talk up your achievements. If you feel uncomfortable doing this, imagine that you're talking about a friend who has had your successes, or pretend that you have a new client (aka you!) and you're relaying all the great things they've done.
- **Feedback time.** This is also your time to give feedback on your role. Would you like to propose changes or improvements to the way you and your manager work together? Are there tools that will help you to do a better job? Can you suggest ways that you could work more efficiently? How are things going with you and your colleagues? Are you generally happy in your role? If not, what do you suggest doing about it? Be mindful of how you deliver all this. You don't want to sound as if you have a long list of complaints and this feedback shouldn't take over the whole review.

- **Promotions and raises.** A review is where you can talk freely about your future. Note that you will generally only be eligible for a promotion or raise if you are well and truly completing all of your current duties to a very high standard, and if there is room for growth within the company's structure and budget. If you want a promotion, show how you're already nailing your current job and explain that you want to remain motivated and committed to the company and, in order to do this, need new challenges. If you feel you deserve a raise, clearly outline the reasons for this and, again, ensure that you link back to how you have benefited the company. If you can demonstrate how you have saved or made the company money, explain this.
- **Goal-setting.** After you've absorbed all that's been said, discuss with your manager what your goals will be over the coming year, and set timelines for them. If you both need to think more about these goals and there's not enough time to do this in your review, ask for a follow-up meeting and schedule it in your calendars while you're still together. If a salary increase or promotion hasn't been possible this time around, ask what steps you will need to take to make this possible so that you know what you need to do. And keep a record of this so that you can bring it up at your next review.
- **Game day.** Treat your review like you would a job interview or important presentation. Practise beforehand by stating all of your feedback and requests out aloud. Ask a trusted friend to listen to you so that you can be confident you're being clear. Get a good sleep the night before and arrive with plenty of time to spare so that you're not feeling flustered. If you are nervous, soothe yourself beforehand with either of the breathing exercises from pages 83–84.

While performance reviews are undeniably important for your career progression, please do remember that **it's what you do every day when you show up for work that's more important**.

Every day of your working life you're on show, so no matter how impressive you are at your performance review, it's what you do on the other 200+ working days in the year that really counts.

Dealing with office politics

Office politics can be tricky.

At any company with different departments and a management hierarchy, there will ALWAYS be some kind of politics at play.

While a company may have an overarching goal, people have their own personal agendas and these can sometimes cause conflicts. Throw a bunch of different personality types into this mix, and it can often feel like it's GAME ON.

Those who are given the great projects or who are promoted aren't always the most skilled, but it's likely they're strategic and good communicators.

> You have a few options:
>
> 1. Pretend that the politics don't exist.
> 2. Fight the politics to try and level the playing field.
> 3. Work it to your personal advantage.
> 4. Work it to both your company's and your own advantage.
>
> The last one is always my choice.

Because politics does exist, and it always will.

Fighting against it will only add to the drama and distract you from your work.

And working it only to your personal advantage will leave you exposed when you demonstrate (rightly or wrongly) that you're not a team player and that you don't care about the company.

So observe your workplace carefully. No matter how big or small the organisation is, get to know all the different people and departments and how they operate individually, as well as how they fit into the company's bigger picture.

Ask questions. Who's making the most profit for your company or bringing in the most business? Who has the most creative ideas? Who has the most industry connections? You'll soon learn where value is placed. When you know what's most valued, you can start to add to that.

You'll also be able to find out who your allies are so that you can work together to continue to add value. From there, you'll be able to identify your champions, who appreciate what you do, and they'll be able to both support you and spread the word about your great work.

A few other tips:

- **Game time.** For many who have the extreme privilege of living in the western world, work – much like life – is all a fabulous game (and I don't mean the Hunger Games). Yes, there will be times when your job and the people you work with are challenging or tedious. But that's all part of the game. And either you're playing or you're not.
- **Personal versus professional.** Learn to separate these when you need to. You won't personally like everyone you have to work with, but you can get along with them professionally instead. If you're a bit of a people pleaser, it can be tough to realise that not everyone is going to like you. Especially when you see those people out socialising together, or interacting on social media and ignoring you. But people are all very different, with unique values and ways of operating. They're not necessarily right or wrong, they're often just different. Take comfort in the fact that if you've never put someone offside before, even by complete accident, it'd mean that you didn't stand for something.
- **No judgement.** There are a couple of people from previous jobs I've had who didn't like to work with me. After losing sleep over this for quite some time, I analysed it and realised that it came down to me being extremely passionate about the project I was working on and them not having the same passion. That's not necessarily a problem, but my thoughtless actions became one. I thought that they were total slackers and I called them out on this. To our boss. Very bluntly. And it damaged their relationship with our boss, and possibly even their career prospects at the time – something I deeply regret. With the benefit of hindsight, I know I would never do this again, even though it had come from pure frustration on my part, or that I would rephrase what I said. It also made me realise that you can't expect everyone to feel the same level of enthusiasm

or passion for your work as you might. And that's okay. Just do the best that you can with the people you have around you. Your work will speak for itself – your bosses aren't idiots.

Fast forward to when I have my own company. I've made it our policy that we don't take on projects unless all those who will be working on it absolutely love it. That way we won't have the same issues that I struggled with.

- **Don't hold grudges.** Trust that people are doing the best they can at any particular moment, with the skills and life lessons they have at that time. Allow others to make their own choices and deal with the consequences, just as you make yours. Also, holding grudges is poisonous and exhausting. Let that sucker go and enjoy how light you feel.
- **Network.** The saying goes, 'If you're the smartest person in the room, you're in the wrong room.' I believe that wholeheartedly. While competency is a nice feeling and there's nothing wrong with enjoying being in a safe space with colleagues or contemporaries who are at your level, if you want to advance your career, you will need to continually put yourself in situations where you don't know what you're doing, which will force you to level up. This will remain the case as you progress. I'm constantly putting myself into networking events or meetings where I'm out of my depth, because I want to be around people whose diversity, intelligence and experience will open my eyes, mind and heart and push me to grow even further. What opportunities do you have to spend time with those smarter than you?
- **Integrity.** The good news is that you don't need to lose this in order to effectively manage those around you – it's not about manipulating people. Build authentic relationships within your organisation and wider industry. You will soon find like-minded people and, together, you'll build influence and power. And when you have this, you can use it to do good.

Bec's touched on office politics already, but it's really important so I'm going to add my take too.

There will always be people in your office who are up for a good bitch. Sometimes this may be vicious, or perhaps it's just a way for them to let off steam. Some people even see it as a way to bond.

If what they're saying is blatantly untrue, by all means challenge them on it. Lies can be really damaging, and everyone deserves to have someone in their corner.

But otherwise, stay out of it when you can. Gossiping puts a lot of stress and negative energy into your day.

It's easy-ish to avoid when your peers are doing it – gently steer the conversation somewhere else, or walk away, or put your headphones on and get back to work.

Easy go-to lines include:

- 'Sorry guys, I love you but I'm out of here. If I'm not contributing positively to the conversation, I don't want to get involved.'
- 'Sorry, I have so much on my plate that I have to get back to work.'
- 'I get it, but I'm trying to stay in a positive headspace so I can't get into this.'
- 'Let's resolve this instead of talking about it behind people's backs.'

One of the magazines I worked at had the most amazing editor – she was brash, funny and so inspiring.

And one of my favourite things about working in that space was that everything was up-front. There was no silly, immature gossiping.

This created a great office culture – if there was an issue you went directly to the person to try to sort it out.

The reason this worked is that the editor led by example. She never entered into a bitchy conversation; she respected others and in turn she was highly respected. So even though it was a high-stress office with tight deadlines, it was so great not having to deal with the politics that can drain so much time and energy.

Listen, act, grow: you may already know a lot when you're starting out in your career. You no doubt have something to contribute, and your fresh take on a situation can lead to startling innovation.

But most of the time, you simply need to learn from those who have gone before you.

It is those who are prepared to listen and take information on board who will go far.

LISTEN,
ACT,
grow.

CHAPTER 10

OVERCOMING SETBACKS & DEALING WITH CHANGE

why this will be your best secret weapon

A lot of bad stuff is going on in the world at the moment.

And the longer you stay in this world, the more likely it is that bad stuff will happen to you (good stuff too, but inevitably also bad stuff).

Before you switch off, thinking you don't need my negativity right now, just hang in there for a second.

I'm much more of a 'glass half full' than a 'glass half empty' kind of person.

Though I'm probably also inclined to describe what the glass looks like and to analyse the taste and smell of the liquid in it, and then to ask where we can get the liquid from . . .

So call me a positive, information-seeking realist.

Bad stuff happens.

You might lose that dream job or client. You might face medical scares, disappointments, relationships dissolving or family members passing away. Not to mention larger-scale social, political and environmental challenges we are all to some extent affected by – terrorism, climate change, natural disasters, pandemics, economic instability . . . the list goes on.

Over the past couple of years my dad and sister have been battling cancer and my mum has had two strokes. This also made them more vulnerable during the coronavirus pandemic. Spending time with them and helping to look after them, plus coming to terms with the idea of losing them, has been a real challenge emotionally, especially as we live in different states.

But I've drawn some advice from a book my brother put me on to years ago. *The Winner's Bible* by neuroscientist Dr Kerry Spackman is a fascinating look at the human mind and how you can actually rewire both your logical and emotional brain circuits to your advantage.

Among other things, Kerry has been a long-term consultant to several Formula One teams, specialising in the performance optimisation of drivers. He also has his head screwed on priority-wise, living an authentic and socially conscious life.

He has a lot to say about overcoming disappointment and disaster; in fact, he's dedicated an entire chapter to it. It's really interesting, can't-put-down stuff, but it's also very detailed and based on medical science, so I'm not going to attempt to summarise it here (but I'd really recommend getting his book and reading it!).

One part that stuck with me was 'Lessons from happy 100-year-olds'.

A study was done to find out the key factors that determine why some people get unwell and die before they're seventy, while others are fit, healthy and happy at one hundred.

They conducted thousands of medical examinations and studied hundreds of factors, including genes, diet, wealth and exercise. The results were extremely surprising. The three factors that stood out above all the others weren't biological (e.g. heart disease, cholesterol or high blood pressure) – they were *thought processes*.

As Kerry explains in his book, this is excellent news because whereas your biology is largely determined by your genes, you can change your thought processes.

> **The study showed that the three most important qualities happy, healthy 100-year-olds have are:**
>
> 1. **an exocentric view of life (one that focuses outwards, not inwards)**
> 2. **a passion that is actively pursued**
> 3. **an ability to get over disappointment.**

Endeavouring to have these three things will no doubt set you up for a happier existence, no matter how long you live for.

Disappointment often leaves us feeling deflated. When things don't turn out the way we want, we can start to feel that they will never go well for us.

But there's another way to look at this. Because the beauty of disappointment, if you choose to see it, is its flip side – while challenging, if you choose to work on it, it eventually offers you a bridge to a nicer, kinder, more peaceful place; somewhere where you can calmly accept the reality you find yourself in; where you value every moment, appreciate the people and things that you do have and take nothing for granted.

The key word here is 'eventually'.

You're not going to be able to overcome a major setback straight away.

That path away from disappointment might feel like a rickety suspension bridge swaying hundreds of metres over a ravine.

You're scared and tired and would rather just dwell in disappointment (and your bed/couch/Netflix) for a while longer.

But dwelling is merely surviving, not living.

So at some point, it's time to begin your journey across.

The first thing to do as you take those hesitant first steps onto the suspension bridge is to grip the ropes on either side of you. They will steady you and stop you from falling. As you take each step – and even when you're sitting down to have a breather – stay hanging on to those ropes.

Those ropes are the other two qualities I mentioned earlier:

- an exocentric view of life – focusing on your family, friends, work colleagues and community
- a passion that is actively pursued – we worked out our passions (or curiosities) in chapter two, so turn to the notes you took.

So whether you're the one currently battling disappointment or the fortunate one who's in a position to assist, incorporating these two factors into your daily life will help you.

There will never be any instant solutions for overcoming adversity, but recognising that your thought processes will either propel you forward to a better place or hold you back in a murkier one is as good a start as any.

> Another thing you should know . . .
>
> It's GOOD TO MAKE MISTAKES!

Um, what?

Seriously, the best thing you can learn is that it's okay to make mistakes.

In fact, it's GREAT to make mistakes!

No-one, I repeat, NO-ONE, knows how to do everything correctly the first time around.

This is important so it's in bold: **Making mistakes is part of the learning experience.**

The process goes:

1. Try really hard at something.
2. Realise that it didn't quite work or wasn't quite right.
3. Find out what you did wrong, correct it, and get straight back up and try again (or retain the information you've gained for the next time this happens again).

Step three is the SUPER crucial one but is where many people fall over because they either:

a. feel so terrible about their 'failure' that they don't try again

OR

b. don't take the time to find out what they did wrong to ensure they don't make the same mistake next time.

How to solve challenge a:

Suck it up. Seriously. Feel bad for a minute, have a cry or a yell or feel anxious – let yourself experience all of those things – but then GET BACK UP.

Your boss might yell at you, you might lose some money you invested, you might have made yourself sick – but this doesn't mean it's the end; it's simply part of a learning process. Experience it, then accept it. (And as we discovered in chapter six, if you choose to reframe any anxiety you're feeling about a lesson you've just learnt as excitement, this will make you a lot happier and more motivated too.)

How to solve challenge b:

To know why something didn't work, you might need to dig to get to the truth. Find someone to help you do this.

The trick is to do this very, VERY graciously. If you just screwed up a work project, chances are your boss is a bit mad because it was an important part of a bigger picture, or it's made them look bad, or it's cost them money.

But find a time to apologise when they're not stressed out of their head, and explain that you made a mistake purely because you didn't know HOW to do it as you hadn't done it before (if this is the case) – not because you were lazy or didn't care. Tell them that you REALLY want to grow from this and make sure you deliver a killer result next time, and ask if they can please explain what was missed, and how you can do better in future. (A sidenote to trying again: if you don't know how to do something, always ask for help or guidance; you obviously shouldn't be tackling an important task without the necessary skills and knowledge.)

Again, the key here is to be respectful of other people's time. While you may have a lot going on in your life, your boss and others more senior and more experienced than you most likely have greater responsibilities in both their professional and personal lives, so they will probably have limited time to help you. So if you're going to talk to them about your mistake, come prepared to explain what went wrong, why you think it went wrong, and what strategies you'll put in place to make sure it doesn't happen again – then, and only then, ask for their advice.

Allowing yourself to make mistakes does NOT mean that you can be slack the first time around. It goes without saying that you should try your very best; if you don't, other people will be less inclined to help you, and they are the ones you'll learn from.

> **The most successful people aren't those who do everything perfectly all the time.**
>
> **The most successful people are those who recover from mistakes the fastest, and who learn from them so that they're not repeated.**

So lose that fear of making a mistake. Instead, channel your energy into asking, 'How can I do the very best I can?'

When you're playing it 'safe' you're not going to be able to grow and move towards that thing you really want.

We all tend to shy away from fear, from the unknown and from making mistakes.

But if you don't know what fear feels like, how will you become fearless?

IF YOU DON'T KNOW WHAT
FEAR FEELS LIKE,
HOW WILL YOU BECOME

fearless?

Future-proofing

We never truly know what the future holds for our careers, especially as the world changes.

But we can try to minimise the effects that any changes may have on us, and that's called future-proofing.

> **This is something your bosses and senior executives likely give a lot of thought to, so if you're interested in progressing your career, it's something that should become important to you too.**

We can't always predict what will happen to the economy and what that will mean for employment. And in coming decades, as tech develops more and more, many jobs will become automated.

But there are skills that will always be needed, no matter what happens. In creative industries, **solving complex problems that involve multiple ideas, communicating with words and images, having a deep knowledge of different cultures, being familiar with new media and tech, and social and emotional intelligence will remain highly desirable.**

So regardless of whether times are amazing or tough, or how tech changes the industries we work in, try to develop these skills.

Also, the following will always be true. To continue to thrive professionally you need:

- to be truly excited about what you do
- to have the skill set to do it to the highest level
- to have a market for your products or services
- to be adding more value than your competitors
- to know more about your customers than anyone else
- to try and predict what your customers need and be ready to serve it to them.

Hit all six of these and you'll have the best possible chance of a life-long, winning career.

When you've had a setback, sometimes you do need to step away from the situation for a while. This is why having a passion that you actively pursue is so important. And while your passion may be the work that you do, it's important to find other things you enjoy too. This all goes towards making sure you don't burn out.

I know that when I spend time in nature, researching new places to travel to, or catching up with other creatives, I get a real sense of fulfilment. Doing these things also helps me to clear my head so I can deal with any not-so-great things that are going on.

One thing to be mindful of when finding a passion is that it doesn't add extra stress, pressure or fatigue.

If you're feeling a bit down and fashion is one of your interests, you might think, 'I'll just do a bit of shopping because I have been working really hard and I deserve it.' But while a spot of retail therapy may feel good in the short term, it's scientifically proven that the relief will be short-lived, and will only leave you craving more (which your bank balance and stress levels won't be thanking you for).

And the same could apply if you're a massive foodie. Sure, it's great to indulge in delicious desserts or get stuck into a cocktail-making class. But you may need to take it easy here as the road to happiness isn't going to be found at the bottom of a box of gourmet doughnuts or a bottle of organic rosé. (Bec here: Couldn't agree more. And I should know – I've tried this many, many times. It. Does. Not. Work.) Yes, most definitely enjoy these things, but try to focus on a passion that will nourish you.

If I don't have time to go hiking or skiing (two of my big loves), I still make time to get outside every day, by going for a walk at the beach or just around my neighbourhood.

And I know that if I avoid spending too much money, I can save all those little bits of cash to pursue my main passions, which will have a much more lasting effect on my happiness.

While I was saving up to work and travel in the US for a year, I found joy in activities that are free. I have worked out that experiences give me so much more joy than 'things'.

But that's just me. What are your passions? Set aside time to immerse yourself in these – whether for an hour or for a whole weekend – then come back to whatever that setback was, and I bet you'll have some fresh perspective on it.

CHAPTER 11

HOW TO BE COOL IN A CRISIS

and how to nip them in the bud

Nobel Prize winner Rudyard Kipling wrote the poem 'If—' around 1895.

The poem remains one of the best and most relevant pieces of advice today – it's worth a read for so many reasons.

Kipling was about thirty years old when he wrote it, inspired by an English nobleman who had led a military mission that was, in many ways, a complete disaster. But this nobleman became a hero for publicly taking complete responsibility for its failure.

'If—' was a favourite of one of my best friends' dads, and was read at his funeral because it truly sums up how he tried (and succeeded) to live his life. It's also a favourite of the awesome Aussie comedian Anh Do – he included it in his brilliant and inspiring autobiography *The Happiest Refugee*.

Anyway, here's the poem (and ladies, feel free to change the last line to '. . . you'll be a queen/Beyoncé').

'If—'

If you can keep your head when all about you
Are losing theirs and blaming it on you,
If you can trust yourself when all men doubt you,
But make allowance for their doubting too;
If you can wait and not be tired by waiting,
Or being lied about, don't deal in lies,
Or being hated, don't give way to hating,
And yet don't look too good, nor talk too wise:

If you can dream – and not make dreams your master;
If you can think – and not make thoughts your aim;
If you can meet with Triumph and Disaster
And treat those two impostors just the same;
If you can bear to hear the truth you've spoken
Twisted by knaves to make a trap for fools,
Or watch the things you gave your life to, broken,
And stoop and build 'em up with worn-out tools:

If you can make one heap of all your winnings
And risk it on one turn of pitch-and-toss,
And lose, and start again at your beginnings
And never breathe a word about your loss;
If you can force your heart and nerve and sinew
To serve your turn long after they are gone,
And so hold on when there is nothing in you
Except the Will which says to them: 'Hold on!'

If you can talk with crowds and keep your virtue,
Or walk with Kings – nor lose the common touch,
If neither foes nor loving friends can hurt you,
If all men count with you, but none too much;
If you can fill the unforgiving minute
With sixty seconds' worth of distance run,
Yours is the Earth and everything that's in it,
And – which is more – you'll be a Man, my son!

While there are so many valuable ideas in this poem worth considering, the focus of this chapter is the opening line – being that person who's calm when everyone around you is losing their head.

As the saying goes, nothing is certain except death and taxes. Which means that change is going to happen.

And that's often all a crisis is – a big change.

And it's not usually comfortable.

If you're going through an incredibly blissful, prosperous, healthy phase, at some point this will change.

If times are stressful, rubbish or dull, this will change too.

Sometimes change is scary, but often it's welcome.

But know this:

> **The choices that we make every single moment of each day determine what will happen next.**

And even when events occur that are out of our control, it's our reaction to them and our attitude that will shape what unfolds.

We all deal with change differently.

I've learnt (through trials, tears, wine, cake and error) that when everything is shifting around me and I'm feeling lost and adrift, creating some sense of familiarity really helps:

- I try to get up and go to bed at the same time each day.
- I eat fresh, nutritious meals at regular intervals.
- I burn a candle or spray a scent with a familiar, comforting smell.
- I talk to family members or long-time friends.
- I cut myself some slack and try not to beat myself up for not having it perfectly together.

I also say to myself, 'Soon you will look back on this time – will you be proud of how you handled the situation?' That question helps me to determine what I'll do next.

Doctor and best-selling author Spencer Johnson gives some very simple advice in his gem of a book *Peaks and Valleys*. It goes something like this:

When life feels like crap:

Take a deep breath, and know that this won't last forever. Focus on doing the opposite of what put you in this position. Don't compare yourself to others, or even to your 'happier' past self. What's the silver lining in this bad time?

When life is fantastic and couldn't be better:

Be humble, gracious and grateful. Do more of what put you in this position. Focus on others and what you can do for them. Save your resources for the crap times ahead.

As a PR professional, working in the fast-paced and high-stakes world of crisis communications is something that I really enjoy.

I've learnt how to step back from a situation, quickly assess what's happening, and work out a way to either solve it or make it less bad. My job then becomes communicating this information to everyone involved – whether in person, on the phone, over email or through the media or social media – so that they all feel as good about the situation as possible.

And in my business, the first hour after a crisis hits is crucial. What happens during this time often determines whether our crisis response will be effective or fail.

It's when the situation is contained and essential facts are gathered that help to shape the next hours or days.

> The best defence in crisis communications is preparedness.
>
> So when a crisis hits, we don't panic.

We keep our cool, gather information, engage as necessary, and leverage that first hour to ensure we are ready to face and manage the crisis ahead and get back to business as quickly as possible.

This is a 10-step PR plan that my team and I at The Comms Department often use for our clients when dealing with a crisis.

It's a very PR- and comms-specific plan, but what's great about it is that you can adapt it to any kind of crisis – whether your boss is driving you insane, there's a family meltdown, you're dealing with illness, or you're having relationship issues, etc. Just swap out a few of the key words and adapt it to your situation (for example, in some cases you may wish to skip steps 8 and 9, which are more media related; and in sections that relate to the media you could swap in 'other parties' instead).

Step 1

Focus on the most immediate and pressing issue and take steps to stop any further damage

It's easy to freak out when something unexpected happens. Your mind can either freeze or go into overdrive thinking of all the terrible scenarios that may unfold because of what's just happened. But step 1 asks you to forget that for the moment. This is where you shake yourself out of it and focus only on what's happened and, if possible, see if you can stop anything else from happening. If there's been an accident, is everyone now out of harm's way? If they're not, can you help to ensure that they are?

Step 2

Contain everyone who's directly involved

Most crises involve several people. Can you get them all together as quickly as possible, whether in person, on a conference call, or in a group chat?

Step 3

Get the facts

What's actually happened? There are facts and there is drama. You need to get past the drama and only look at the cold, hard facts.

Step 4

Identify the impact

This is the damage or fallout from what's occurred. How bad is it really? Again, be realistic in your assessment, not dramatic. Then analyse if it has the potential to become worse.

Step 5

Determine who else is involved and who needs to be and bring them together immediately

Whereas in step 2 we brought together everyone *directly* involved, this time we look more broadly. Imagine that a really nasty and completely untrue email about you or your company was sent to a huge group of journalists and was forwarded to you. In addition to contacting your boss and everyone else directly involved, you'd likely bring together executives such as the PR Director, the CMO and possibly the COO and CEO to brief them on what's happened and what the plan is to fix it.

Step 6

Know where the media (or other parties) stands

When crises occur, there are usually people who either want or need to know what's happened (such as the media, if the crisis is newsworthy), as well as those directly affected. Who are these people and how do they currently feel about the situation? This step may involve assessing content posted online, or having phone calls or immediate in-person conversations. You may not make an official statement just yet, as you're seeking information about people's thoughts on the crisis. (Note that before you do speak to anyone, you may need to have a 'holding statement' handy – see the next step for more detail.)

Step 7

Work out the message and determine who the key spokesperson will be

Now that you know what's happened, have contained it as best you can, know what the damage is, have talked to those involved and those who need to know, AND know what others think about it, it's time to start communicating more broadly. In previous steps we gathered information and had internal discussions, but now it's time to prepare to deliver your message to a wider audience. Who do you need to communicate with to attempt to repair this problem, what are you going to say, and who's going to say it? (Note that as with most rules, there is an exception to this one – if it's going to take a long time to get to this step, you may need to start communicating sooner rather than later. Because if you say nothing for a very long time, people will start to make up their own stories about what happened, and they won't necessarily be factual. So you may want to provide a 'holding statement', which may be as simple as, 'I realise that this is potentially serious and I'm looking into it. As soon as it's been investigated fully, I'll come back to you.')

Step 8

Respond or make an official statement to the media and/or other parties who may be involved

Depending on your situation, you may or may not need to speak to the media at this point. Continue to assess the situation. If you do need to speak to the media, read page 170 of chapter fourteen, 'PR & comms tools', where I give you my proven tips for working with journalists.

And if you're not talking to the media, who else – more broadly again – needs to be informed or reassured? What is the best way to communicate with them? In person, on the phone, or using email?

Step 9

Monitor coverage in the media and on social media, assess it, then plan your response

If coverage has escalated and the crisis is now being talked about on social media, consider whether you need to address it there too. If so, who should be doing the talking?

Meanwhile, keep monitoring the situation – is it getting better or worse? What more can you do to fix it? Perhaps it needs to play out for a short period of time (even if it's painful) so that everyone who feels they need to weigh in on it can – but then after that's happened, you can all move on. (In this fast-moving world, there's always another news event that will come along and remove the focus from yours!)

Step 10

Debrief

This takes place when things have calmed down – when the crisis has been averted or run its course. This is where you work out exactly how it happened and what you can do to try to make sure it doesn't happen again. You should also review how you handled steps 1–9 – is there anything you could have handled better that you can learn from for next time?

The excellent thing about crises is that – provided you learn from them – the more of them you experience, the better you will become at dealing with them.

If you only take away one thing from this chapter, make it what was mentioned in step 3 of our PR crisis plan: learn to distinguish facts from drama.

> Facts are reality.
>
> Drama is a choice.

In my early twenties, I definitely skewed more towards drama when something terrible happened. And this always made things worse.

The problem in front of you is enough to deal with.

Adding *your reaction* to it only leads to more complications and stress.

Over time, with determination and practice, I learnt how to step back from a situation and observe and assess it before responding. This skill not only makes you less stressed because you know how to calm a crisis, but it also makes you more strategic. It's a skill that will serve you very well in any professional environment as it's something that your bosses and clients will value and notice.

Meditating regularly has also seriously increased my ability to be cool in a crisis as well as my ability to empathise and connect with people. And don't just take my word for it – meditation has been around for thousands of years but now science has caught up and proven its benefits.

Recently, after I had steered a client through a huge crisis for their company, the exhausted but happy Managing Director turned to me and said, 'I want to call you the Ice Queen for how cool you were during that crisis but that's not the right name because you were also so warm and thoughtful when looking after me and my staff.' That comment is one of the greatest compliments I've ever received, especially because I used to be the other kind of royalty . . . a Drama Queen!

I'm telling you this because if I can change, anyone can. And in addition to having a crisis plan, perhaps consider looking into meditation or other mindfulness practices – the benefits may astound you.

How to avoid a deadline freak-out

Deadlines are part of being a designer but, as an anxious person, having a deadline thrust upon me from out of the blue used to send me into a spiral. Here are some tips for avoiding stress while managing deadlines:

- Do one task at a time – don't jump all over the place or you won't get anything finished.
- Make a list and number the tasks in order of priority and work through them in that order. Don't make this list crazy long or you will be overwhelmed. List four items at most and you will feel great when you check these off. Another trick is to estimate how long it will take to do each task and to write this next to the task. Adding these times up will give you a better idea of what you can realistically achieve in a day.
- Don't get distracted. I know it's easy when you are under pressure to think of a million other little things you need to do. But just start the project!
- If it's not a surprise assignment, give yourself an early deadline so that if any issues arise you still have plenty of time. Always aim to complete the job prior to the deadline.
- Write yourself a list at night, then get up fresh and early to start on it and you will get the job completed much faster. I find that things always seem far worse at night, and that I am more creative in the morning. If you're more of a night person, still work on that list so that you know what needs to be accomplished. Perhaps you'll even cross a few things off that evening. But do make sure you get some sleep! And then, in the morning, you'll have your list ready to guide you.
- Breathe. Just breathe.

BE THE PERSON
WHO'S
calm
WHEN EVERYONE
AROUND YOU IS
LOSING THEIR HEAD

CHAPTER 12

STARTING YOUR OWN BUSINESS

top tips to drive your success

Congratulations!

Perhaps you've reached the stage where you want to take a leap of faith, or you've realised that after many years of training and experience, you're ready to launch out on your own.

Maybe you want to start a serious side hustle.

We're all different, but in my experience, there is honestly nothing more professionally satisfying than running your own show.

And with today's technology allowing you to connect directly with your customers, it's never been easier to start a business.

But know this:

- The buck will end with you. If the business fails, that will be on you; but if it's a huge success, that success is also yours.
- There will be times when you'll question what on earth you were thinking and you'll want to quit.
- You will have to work harder than you ever have in your whole life.
- Managing people will probably be the most unpredictable and challenging part of your job – but the relationships you'll develop with incredible people will probably be your greatest reward.

So what's your business?

> It is useless being the most creative, original, daring and hardworking professional if you can't sell what you create.

After you've established that what you're planning on doing is in line with your values and that you're truly passionate about it, you need to ask yourself some questions:

1. Does the world need this service?

- If the answer is NO, then it won't work. Back to the drawing board.
- If the answer is YES, ask yourself the following question.

2. Who are the people that need it and am I in a position to help them?

- Know your audience. If your aim is to grow a large business, there will need to be a lot of people who require your service. Or you will need to be prepared to diversify your offering to help a broader group of people. Diversifying will also limit your risk if a particular industry falls into challenging times, as many did during the 2020 coronavirus pandemic, which severely affected international travel, entertainment, hospitality, physical retail and many other industries.

- Consider whether you are set up to engage with your audience in the way that you need to. Do you have the necessary skills? Are you living in the right city? If you're confident that you can work from a different city, what arrangements will you need to make?

3. Can I provide this product or service in a better or different way to others who are already providing it?

- You need a strong answer here, and I would suggest talking to people you trust who won't be financially affected by your starting a business (as sometimes those well-meaning people will err on the side of caution and say it's all too risky. It's not that they're not being supportive of you, it's usually just that they're worried for you.). The people you speak to should also know you well and understand your industry and why you think you can do this. If they agree, you're probably on the right track. If they look doubtful, ask more people. If they look doubtful too, you may not have found the solution yet.
- An unwavering belief in yourself helps here, as can strong anxiety that your business will fail. For me, it was (and often still is) all about the anxiety, so I made it work for me. As we discussed in chapter six, hijack that fear and turn it into excitement and then use that momentum to spur you on.

How do you set up your business?

Once you can clearly and honestly answer all these questions, you can move on to more practical things such as creating a business plan and working out how you'll finance it.

If your eyes just glazed over when you read that, or you thought, 'I don't know how to do those things – perhaps this isn't for me after all', think again.

No-one who hasn't been to business school knows how to do these things.

Identify all the things you don't know. Embrace them, in fact.

Often they'll be things such as managing finances, getting insurance, marketing, trademarking, securing an office space, or employment laws for hiring staff. You'll need to get some advice here, ideally from a mentor or another business owner, as you won't know what you don't know.

You may be familiar with some of these things but may not *like* to do them.

In the early stages of setting up a business, when money may be tight, I'd encourage you to do all you can by yourself and outsource everything else. An expert will do a better job of some of these things than you will and this will allow you to focus your energy on growing your business faster.

I was never that interested in maths. But if you want to run a business, you need to get good at it.

Sure, I could have just hired someone to manage all the financials for me and blindly let them tell me what to do, but that's an incredibly dangerous situation to put yourself in. What if that person gets busy and your company's needs slip through the cracks? What if something unexpected happens? What if they become sick? What if they're dishonest?

I have a great accountant and bookkeeper and often call on a business consultant for financial advice. Initially I had no idea that these kinds of consultants existed in my industry, or that they would be affordable for a new business like mine. I met my consultant at an industry networking event and what she has taught me has helped me to make operational changes and put procedures in place that have significantly boosted the commercial success of my business. That's meant that I can give salary increases and bonuses to the entire team and hire even more incredible staff. So with help from her and my accountant, I worked really hard to upskill and become proficient enough to really know my numbers. And the better I became at that, the better I became at empathetically engaging with our big corporate clients, especially the all-important CFOs and CEOs who ultimately decide if their companies keep working with us.

> Once you've worked out how you'll operate and finance your business, remember to always keep these three points front and centre:
>
> - Be of service.
> - Be adaptable.
> - Put the customer first.

When you're bogged down in budgets, following up new leads and doing the actual day-to-day work, it's very easy to forget that these three things are the secret to staying in business.

Your health

The first year that The Comms Department was in business was one of the most thrilling of my life.

I could make my own decisions about the kind of work I'd take on and could run the business according to my own strengths and passions – I called all the shots.

But I discovered that, rather than having one boss like I did in my old job, I had about ten. They were called my clients.

I was at their beck and call, trying to make sure they were happy.

And because I wanted to make a name for myself and for the work to be so good it'd speak for itself, I did whatever it took to do an incredible job for them.

This meant that I was working more than a hundred hours a week.

Some weeks I was averaging four hours of sleep a night.

I was eating every meal at my desk.

I had no social or family life.

This was all leading to one thing – burnout.

I won't lie.

At about the three year mark, I almost lost it.

I was physically and emotionally exhausted. I was beginning to get little colds and flus that I couldn't shake, and this weird red rash around my eyes that wouldn't go away. I was short-tempered, disinterested and disengaged from my home-life (cue my poor husband tiptoeing around me, not sure if I was made of steel or fragile glass, and putting his hand up for more and more work trips away, mostly because I was completely ignoring him). I was running a team of people who, although brilliant, each had their own agendas and goals, which meant that I was always the one left carrying the bag if work wasn't done correctly. And I will be the first to admit that I wasn't equipped back then to be solely responsible for, and to truly lead, a team of people.

One afternoon at about 3 pm, after a day in which silly, frustrating mistakes for different clients had piled on top of each other, and on me, I reached the point of being utterly overwhelmed.

I was catatonic. I couldn't even speak.

And although I had a million things to do, I stepped away from my desk and went for a walk.

I needed some air.

Given there had been no time for lunch, I think the aim was to get something to eat.

> It ended with me sitting in a gutter behind a cafe, clutching a takeaway container of salad, as I howled and sobbed down the phone to a friend. I told her I was shutting up shop. That was it. Screw my team, screw my clients, screw the business, I was done.

I swore, cried, gasped for air, yelled, swore a lot more and then finally stopped.

Thankfully, after getting it all out (to that girlfriend I'll be forever grateful to), I realised that I didn't want to give it all away. But serious changes had to be made.

And I realised that reaching that moment of crisis was actually a good thing.

But only so long as I learnt from it.

My first step was to give myself enough time and space each day to get my health back on track.

And this meant I had to learn how to set a lot of boundaries.

Next I had to develop faith that my long-time clients knew they were in safe hands and that, unless there was a critical issue, I didn't need to reply to them instantly night and day (those clients shake their heads and laugh about this today, wondering why I didn't know that all along. It was a good lesson for a perfectionist to learn – not to be so hard on yourself.).

And I spent a huge amount of time reading books on leadership.

> One of the hardest parts of the whole experience was admitting to my team that I wasn't invincible.
>
> I had to be really vulnerable and explain to them what was going on.
>
> It ended up being the best thing ever.

Together, we evolved so that the workload was more evenly spread and we had better internal communication strategies in play, and we were more upfront with clients about whether we could actually meet their expectations within their budgets.

Six months later, we rebranded as a much more evolved and collaborative The Comms Department, and the transformation was complete.

The team and I, along with every new team member who's joined us since, have also made the commitment that as a business we'll always keep learning and evolving, so that we can serve our clients exceptionally well while also having satisfying careers and happy home lives.

Sure, there are still tough days, long hours and moments of utter frustration, but these are always backed by the thought that 'this will pass, and there's light at the end of the tunnel'.

And we'll get to a weekend or a holiday and realise that we're a bit over-tired, but that we ultimately love what we do and, after a short rest, we're excited to get back to it.

Meanwhile, I'm also delighted to report that, since then, the breakdown tally has been zero.

My health has returned to peak form. In fact, thanks to better prioritising, being more efficient, and allowing more hours for exercise, sleep and self-care, I'm probably healthier now than I ever have been.

And less-stressed Bec returned, which meant that my relationship with my hubby went back to its happy normal. Phew. (Though, sidenote: I'm glad we went through that experience because from it we also worked out that since we spend a lot of time away from one another due to work, we need to make more of an effort to stay in touch while we are away. Then, when we are together at home, we focus on being more mindfully present with one another. That way we're not leading separate lives that run a greater risk of drifting apart. Aren't the lessons that come out of challenging times amazing?)

INGA'S TIPS

Six lessons for starting a business:

1. Know that there will be a lot of work involved and that you need to be really passionate about it.
2. It can take a long time to build momentum, so you have to be patient.
3. Start simple. Don't get caught up with grand marketing plans or tools that cost a lot of money. Word of mouth is free.
4. You are your own boss, which is amazing, and you are in full control of how you spend your time. However, know that there will be certain periods when you have to put in long hours to make a project deadline, and that sometimes projects will be guided more by the client.
5. Find a good accountant and use a program such as Xero or Myob – these are game changers.
6. Create work and get it out there, even when you don't have a client project at hand. You want people to be seeing and talking about your work. When I was in the US I was busy with client work but also wanted to spend time on some creative projects that were just for me. I started drawing houses I liked at night and popping them on Instagram. These seemed to really resonate with people and this is now another arm of my business as I get lots of commissions to draw homes.

   Check them out here:

   inkling_house

PREPARE TO WORK

harder

THAN YOU EVER
HAVE BEFORE

CHAPTER 13

OTHER LIFE LESSONS

that will greatly help you
in your professional life

Bec's tips:

- **Focus.** In today's world, focus is as important as intelligence. Thanks to the internet, we have easy access to information that will allow us to do just about anything. And if we can't physically do it ourselves, we can easily connect with someone who can. So knowledge clearly isn't the problem when it comes to getting things done. But focus is. How can you better prioritise the tasks that need your time and your committed attention?
- **Transformation is hard.** We all see so many 'success' stories in the media about entrepreneurs under thirty making it big. Or unicorn startups that are now valued in the millions. Kylie Jenner is already a billionaire. You need to know that this is extraordinary and that while these are inspiring and possibly even motivating stories, they are not the norm. Success always requires a certain amount of luck – whether that's timing or being connected to the right person or family (such as having Kim Kardashian as your sister and Kris Jenner as your mum). But more than just luck, transformation is hard. Really hard! So if on your path towards that thing you want you feel inadequate, challenged, and like you'll never get it right . . . that's 100 per cent normal. Just embrace that it's difficult, because once you stop fighting that fact, there's one less challenge in your way.

  Recognising that it's hard can also lighten up a tricky situation and boost your mood, which in turn makes the work more enjoyable. I heard a great interview with Jess and Stef Dadon, fashion personalities, bloggers and founders of the super successful TWOOBS brand, on Heather Maltman's *One Together* podcast. I highly recommend listening to the whole thing, but, in summary, the Dadon sisters talked about learning how to run their amazing business. One point that they made was that when they're in a really serious and intense situation, one of them will turn to the other and exclaim, 'Business is HARD!' And that moment of admitting it takes the edge off. It makes them laugh and removes the expectation that they have to know all this stuff. In their words, 'It's become this thing we say all the time . . . it just puts it into perspective, it makes it hilarious. It's such a dumb sentence but it's real though, it *is* hard!' And after that moment, with a lighter, more positive mindset, they roll their figurative sleeves back up and get back to work. And if these savvy sisters can acknowledge that it's hard, and laugh about it, so can we.

- **You are responsible for how you react.** If you are feeling frustrated or annoyed, it's up to you to change this. Yes, someone may have been a complete pain in the ass and said something to provoke you, but you are ultimately in control of your mindset, and because you can choose how you react to the provocation, this makes it oh so much easier to let it go.
- **Stoicism and resilience.** Also known as the 'suck it up and stick with it' combo. These are two of the greatest and most overlooked qualities you can develop. Stoicism is developing mental toughness and acknowledging that while you can't always prevent bad things from happening, you can certainly always try to deal with them without getting worked up. If something's challenging, can you reframe how you're looking at it? And can you put any negativity aside for the moment, and just get on with dealing with it? I see a lot of these two qualities in my parents, and in those over the age of 70 who have been through a lot in life. They don't complain – it is what it is – they just get on with it. But anyone at any age can benefit from being more stoic. Meanwhile, resilience is the ability to cope when things go wrong and to bounce back afterwards. Have another read of chapter ten, 'Overcoming setbacks & dealing with change', for some pointers.
- **The ego is the enemy.** One of the secrets to being a great PR is to check your ego at the door. When you're working with big companies or brands, you're likely already dealing with some powerful people, often with matching egos. Once you remove yours from the equation, everything becomes a lot simpler. That doesn't mean becoming a doormat for everyone to walk over – you still have a lot to contribute and you need to ensure that people are taking you seriously. But don't allow your own sense of self to become so inflated that you start to make the situation more complicated. Make it all about the work, not about you. Have poise, don't pose. *Ego Is the Enemy* is also the title of a Ryan Holiday book mentioned in chapters nine and sixteen.
- **Watch your mouth.** Great PRs are always known as 'The Vault' because we know how to keep information private. So try not to gossip, and don't talk loudly about your clients/boss/colleagues/business partners in public. If you need to discuss them, use a code name. Ears are everywhere and many a promising professional career has been cut down thanks to someone running their mouth in public.

- **Collaborate.** When you have your head down working, it's easy to get a little professionally isolated. So it's important to factor in time for meetings with other people – mentors, entrepreneurs and others in the industry. Can you find a great networking group that suits your personality and budget? Future Women and Business Chicks are two great organisations in Australia, though there are many others out there too. Try to maintain regular contact with those who are smarter and more accomplished than you so that you can grow – this is something you should try to do your whole life, no matter if you're at the very top of your field.
- **The obstacle is the way.** The problem doesn't have to be a problem. Not only can a problem be an opportunity for growth, it can actually be the best way forward. (*The Obstacle Is the Way* is also the title of another great book by Ryan Holiday – more on this in chapter sixteen, 'Books I love'.)
- **Get up, dress up, show up.** All the pre-planning, positivity and creative and strategic genius in the world is always beaten by the person who makes it there on the day. Look, I get it. Sometimes you just can't be bothered showing up somewhere. Often you've worked so hard in the lead-up to the 'thing' (perhaps a test, interview, meeting or event) that, by the time it arrives, you're either a bit over it or daunted by it (or both). I've lost track of the amount of times I've woken up and thought, 'I can't do this, I don't want to go.' Maybe it's because my skin has broken out or my clothes don't feel like they fit properly, often because I've had no time to exercise or have been stress-eating. Or I'm run-down and just feel totally meh. There have also been times where self-doubt has crept in, where I feel like I'm not prepared and am tempted to self-sabotage. So many people fall over at this crucial stage, but this is when you:

  - Get up – no texting or phoning in your excuses
  - Dress up – make an effort; have a shower, do your hair, put some make-up on
  - Show up – do the damn 'thing'.

  And by doing it, you advance. Plus, once you're there, it's almost never as awful as it was in your head.

  A concept I learnt from working in show business is that no matter what happens before a performance, when you're a professional, the show must always go on. If there's something bothering you, you need to put it aside and get up and perform. Only once the performance is done can you sort everything else out.

A sidenote: if you see me out and about wearing really bright lipstick, there's a fifty-fifty chance that I've been having one of these meh days and I put a bold lip on after having a stern word with myself to 'dress up!'

GET UP,
DRESS UP,

show up

- **Live more with less** – I have found that by having less I am less overwhelmed and stressed. I have more time to pursue what really makes me happy and this is then reflected in my creative work. Less clutter around me means less clutter in my head.
- **Don't be afraid to speak up** – if you really believe in something but feel a little shy or think it might be silly to speak, don't bite your tongue. Let the other person know what you are thinking in a kind and honest way. You will have no regrets and you should always trust your gut.
- **Never tear others down** – this is something I am really passionate about. I cannot stand hearing other creatives mouthing off about someone else's work. Whether these comments come from jealousy or a desire to gain a competitive edge, all they do is make you look bad. There is enough work for everyone and the more you support others in your industry, the more positive energy will come back to you.
- **If you have a deadline, stick to it** – if those I'm working with aren't reliable or accountable for a project, I won't work with them again. I need to know that they have things under control.
- **Listen** – learn from those who have done this before.
- **Believe in yourself** – don't let that self-doubt creep in. This is a hard one and still happens to me after years in the industry. Work hard, do the right thing and trust yourself. You've got this.

CHAPTER 14

PR & COMMS TOOLS

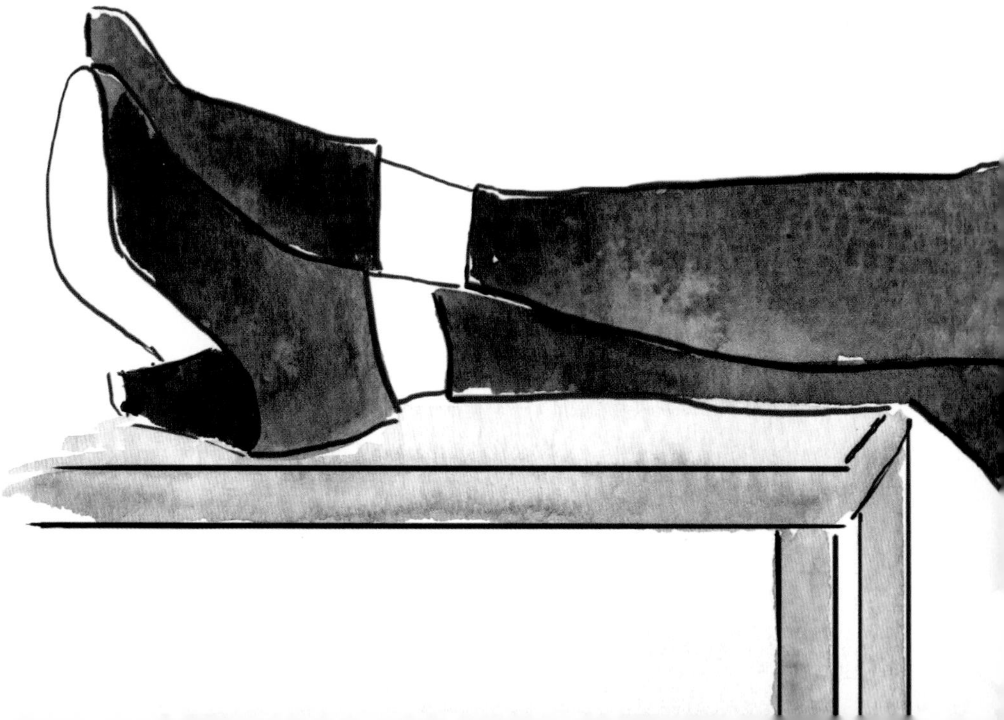

This part of the book is for all you comms and PR stars out there.

But even if you don't work in this industry, this chapter will give you practical tips on how to best work with the media to promote your business or side hustle.

It's stuff that:

- I wish they taught me in uni
- actually works – my PR company's success in securing media coverage for clients and ensuring excellent long-term relationships with journalists has been built from some of these things.

But first, here's a little speculation about the future of our industry.

In five years we won't be working the same way, and it's hard (but fun) to predict what that future looks like.

We do know that the audiences our clients need to speak to are already hugely fragmented.

Back in the old days, if you could get your client on a major TV show, on radio, on the cover of a magazine and in a major newspaper, your job was often done, because most of the country saw that media.

These days, that may be one teeny, tiny part of a PR campaign.

That's because, as consumers, we're all over the place.

Yes, we may be listening to the radio, watching TV or reading the paper, but we're also on mobiles, tablets and laptops. We're on apps, websites and social media.

Online content will flourish, but who creates and controls it? We're using voice-activated devices more than ever – how will this change how we consume content?

We know that social media will only grow, but which platforms will triumph? And how do we communicate with users if there's more of a trend towards private messaging?

Virtual reality, augmented reality and artificial intelligence will bring us far from where we are today, but where will this all land and how will we be using it?

And what about traditional media – radio is looking strong thanks to its investment in podcasts, the desire for local content, the fact that we're still driving cars, and the connection listeners have to on-air talent. But will anything change when self-driving cars come into play and we're free to do other things while we travel?

Though some free-to-air TV networks have been a little shaky, local news and sport currently play a big role in their continued success. And they're all investing in streaming services.

Meanwhile, many media outlets are becoming multimedia owners, with TV or radio now only one part of their business. Print magazines and newspapers will continue to consolidate and will likely become increasingly niche and bespoke.

> **What we do know is this: to remain in business, we need to be ready for change.**

A generation ago, Kodak was one of the world's biggest companies. They primarily sold film for cameras. Thanks to the power of their brand and marketing, the world knew that a 'Kodak moment' was a precious event to be captured and savoured. But Kodak was so blinded by its success as the market leader that it wasn't ready for change or willing to adapt. Cameras went digital, and then were suddenly embedded in everyone's smartphones. And people were happy to share their photos digitally or on social media rather than just printing them. Kodak's competitors pivoted to meet the market's new demands. Kodak didn't and their business collapsed. What a lesson to us all.

Here's what makes me excited.

Truths:

- People will always need to communicate clearly to others. And many people aren't that good at this; but we're the experts and can help.
- People will always want to hear, read or watch stories, and we are the experts at creating them, especially for commercial use.

> **Ultimately, being a skilled communicator and being innovative, nimble and ready for change is what will set you apart in the coming years.**

BE OF

service

How to be a great PR that both clients and the media love to work with

PR is a service industry.

We are here to serve our clients and to serve the media.

If you constantly come back to this and focus on providing the very best service, you will be unbeatable.

And even if you don't work in PR, this advice will help you to be a source journalists like working with, which may mean great media stories for your business and repeat coverage.

Firstly, what is a journalist looking for? It's good to know straight up that:

- What a journalist wants is not always what you want.
- Journalists are rarely interested in helping you (because that's not their job).

Ultimately, they want A GOOD STORY.

This is something that adds value to their audience's lives, and may:

- be entertaining – funny, absurd, heartwarming or salacious
- be educational – something that informs the reader/listener/viewer and makes them feel included and 'in the know'
- get the media clicks (which is why a hot headline can help, as can a compelling story with enough substance to make the audience read, listen to or watch the entire piece, and not turn to something else).

When approaching media:

- Be of service. They are doing you a favour by running a story that includes you or your client, not the other way around.
- Do your research first. Get to know the media outlet and the kinds of stories they publish or broadcast. Is what you want to pitch to them suitable? What politics are at play within that outlet? Who are they owned by and how might this bias or influence their take on the story? Research individual journalists too – is this the kind of story they'd usually cover?
- Be specific. Design a pitch that is 100 per cent tailored to them, so that it suits their media outlet and audience. Long gone are the days of a mass one-size-fits-all media release, unless it's critical news that everyone wants to know about (such as a medical breakthrough, major celebrity

news, important breaking news, or a statement addressing an issue that a large number of journalists have been asking you about).

- Email them if possible (this is usually best) so that they have all the info in front of them.
- Call them if you need to (this is fine too) but make sure you also have an email ready for them as they'll likely ask you to shoot it straight through if they're interested. Don't call them when they're on deadline or right before or during their show. And unless you have the most fascinating breaking news ever, don't call them repeatedly. No one likes a pesky PR.
- Don't send an email in the morning and immediately follow up with a phone call to 'see if they've received it'. They are too busy for this. If they have received it and are interested, they will come back to you.
- Try to provide photos and/or videos for stories. Can you create, supply or arrange what's needed if they want their own photo shoot, such as organising the location, talent and any props? If you're supplying photos, they need to be as high-res as possible, and send them via Dropbox or a similar platform so that you don't clog up the person's inbox with a 20 MB email. Unless this has been agreed upfront, you won't get to approve photos from their photoshoot. And unless it's a paid piece, you also won't get to approve the story before it runs, so don't ask.
- Understand the difference between an exclusive and a first run. If you offer a journalist an exclusive, it means that they are the only media outlet you're giving the story, angle or interview to. If you're offering a first run, you're letting them run the story, angle or interview before you let other media outlets run it.
- Don't ask them about the run date of the story or if they can send you a clipping – it is up to you to keep track of this.

One of the reasons PR is so effective is that it's proven to be more convincing and believable than a paid advertisement. So use this to full effect where you can. Don't forget to optimise – if your client takes out a paid ad, ask if you can integrate it into an editorial feature. But, again, you will need to do this upfront and via the right channels. An editor is not going to take kindly to you telling them that they must run a story because you have an ad spend with their sales department.

Over time you will build relationships with journalists. If you become known to them as someone who provides relevant content that their audience loves, if you deliver photos, audio or video in the format they require, and if you're transparent and honest in your dealings with them, they will enjoy working with you and you'll become a valuable asset to them. Which means that each time they see your name in their overflowing inbox, or they see that you're the one calling them, they will prioritise you.

Media interviews 101

How to deliver a fantastic media interview

Here are some straightforward tips you can pass on to your client before they do an interview (that will make them think you're amazing). Alternatively, if you're the one who'll be in the hot seat, familiarise yourself with these before your big moment.

From the minute you are in the presence of a journalist to the minute you leave, everything you say and do can be reported on. You're on show and on the record the entire time, so be mindful of this.

But also know that **you're the one in control**. The journalist or presenter may be asking the questions, but it's you who can steer the conversation to where you want to take it:

1. In advance, decide on your key messages about the project. Make sure they are also in line with your overall brand.
2. Turn them into succinct sentences and practise saying them out loud.
3. Keep your tone and content interesting and uplifting.
4. Forget about 'speaking to the masses' and focus on speaking to just one person. Have a conversation with the interviewer, but know that their target audience is listening.

> Be wary of giving information 'off the record'. Unless you have a close, trusting personal relationship with this particular journalist, always assume that everything you say will be on the record.

DO:

- Explain yourself – always assume that your interviewer and their readers/listeners/viewers don't know anything about you. Start from scratch, which may mean explaining any backstories. Even if the journalist knows these things, their audience probably doesn't, and the journalist needs it in your words, so tell them.

- Be concise AND interesting – chances are, there's not a lot of print space or airtime for your interview, so make sure what you're saying can be succinctly explained in a couple of sentences. It's great to have additional stories ready in case there's time to tell them, provided they're interesting, informative and pertain to your key messages – they will make you an entertaining interviewee and you'll be someone the media will want to speak to again.
- Maintain eye contact with your interviewer.
- Speak clearly and articulately.
- Be yourself – but an upbeat version of yourself. People want to be inspired, entertained or informed (or all three), and they won't be if your delivery is flat.

DON'T:

- Expect the interviewer to lead you in the direction you want to go in. Remember, the interviewer generally won't care about your key messages, and they may have their own agenda, so you need to be conscious of guiding them.
- Give yes or no answers or expect the interviewer to keep asking questions – engage in the conversation as much as you can.
- Swear or say 'like', 'um', 'what not', 'you know', 'pretty much', 'basically', 'etc etc' too much; and, if possible, try to avoid overusing clichés such as 'at the end of the day' or 'in a nutshell'.
- Touch your hair, jewellery, clothes or face – keep your hands in your lap or on the table in front of you. If you're holding your microphone, keep it still.
- Let anything come out of your mouth that you don't want taken out of context. Period.
- Be late. Ever. Always arrive by your call time, and if you think you'll be late, phone your publicist straight away so they can smooth things over for you. If you're working with the journalist directly, let them know.

How to manage controversial or off-target interview questions and swing the interview around so you're in control

This applies when you're asked something that will steer you away from your key messages or something that you don't really want to talk about. It may also apply when a journalist becomes aggressive in their questioning or tone.

- Never lie. If possible, don't say 'no comment' as this can often imply guilt (even if unfairly).
- Keep it friendly. Try not to go on the defensive. Instead, make the choice not to be baited, which is a tactic some interviewers use to provoke an inflamed or sensationalised response from their interviewees.
- Your best armour is openness and honesty. Don't be flippant or sarcastic – just be polite in your own way then move on by talking about one of your key messages.
- If you don't know an answer, or don't want to answer, never shut the interviewer down. Offer another comment or question instead to keep the conversation flowing and, if you can, come back to your key messages.

> Good phrases you can use to turn the conversation back around include:
>
> - 'Funnily enough . . .'
> - 'It's interesting that you've asked that because what we've found is . . .'
> - 'What a great question, you know it reminds me of . . .'
> - 'Would you mind if I just add . . .'
> - 'Before we get off that subject, let me add . . .'
> - 'That's very interesting, but just before we go on . . .'
> - 'And while <insert what the interviewer just started talking about here> is important, don't forget that . . .'
> - 'Thank you, I can understand why you've asked that and it's great that you're so interested. But as the answer is complex we don't have time to fully get to it today. Though what I can say is . . .'

- And remember, the microphones (and probably also the cameras) are always on, even when the interview looks like it has ended.

Tips for different media

Sometimes the way you or your client deliver an interview will change slightly depending on whether a media story will be written or broadcasted. You can use the following tips or pass them on to your client when you're preparing them for the interview.

For print or online interviews:

- Avoid being too sarcastic or joking too much as when the words are written down they won't always reflect the tone of your voice – this is a really dangerous way to be quoted.
- If you don't want it written, don't say it. If you joke about another brand being terrible, for example, chances are the media will take that quote out of context and run with it.
- Publications can easily distort your words, either on purpose (sadly) or by accident (due to journalists having less time to edit thanks to tighter deadlines). So be clear in what you're saying the first time around.
- If the journalist is happy to receive your comment via email, this is a good idea. That way you can supply your best crafted response rather than something that has slipped out of your mouth by mistake.

For telephone or recorded interviews (to be printed, published online or broadcasted):

- Assume that the tape is rolling from the second you pick up the phone.
- While you're talking to just one person and probably being very familiar with them, assume that you are always being heard by many (as you would be in a radio interview). Again, if you don't want anything written or heard, don't let it come out of your mouth.
- For an interview that will be broadcasted, review all the tips in chapter six, 'Sound'.

For television or filmed interviews:

- Again, review all the tips in chapter six.
- Check how you're sitting or standing and, as you're speaking, be mindful of how you use your eyes, your hands and your smile.
- Keep your energy levels up when you're talking. Don't be too passive in your speech or body language as this can come across as boredom. Remain alert and engaged throughout the interview.
- Always assume that the cameras are rolling and the microphones are live. In a pre-recorded interview, the cameras usually keep rolling after the interview 'ends', and that's often when media will get the off-the-cuff gold they really want. So stay 'on' until you leave.
- Use the interviewer's name and maintain eye contact with them when they're speaking.

For social media or YouTube:

- Think twice before you publish anything, as whatever you publish can stay online forever.
- Don't think that you're talking to some huge, unknown mass. Imagine that you're texting a friend who's in your target demographic. This will ensure that your message cuts through personally to the individual who's reading or watching it.
- Avoid being too cryptic and not providing enough information (unless this is a teaser plan and part of your overall PR strategy!), as people will likely just think you're being attention-seeking or odd. Remember, you're there to be informative, entertaining and interesting (sometimes all three at once).

YOU'RE THE

one

IN CONTROL

CHAPTER 15

DESIGN TOOLS

Inga here.

I couldn't let the PRs have all the fun! So here are some tips for all you design stars too . . .

Some tips to keep both you and your clients happy

As designers we usually have an aesthetic that pleases us, or a really strong style. This is a great thing to have but when working with clients it can sometimes come under strain as your client may have their own ideas about how things should look.

Hopefully the client has come to you after seeing your previous work and knows your style. But they may still present ideas that don't really sit well with you or that throw your creative process out a little (in fact, some ideas are really ghastly and completely out of date!).

It is all about managing expectations and guiding your client through the process:

- The first thing you should do is hold a briefing meeting about the project. By talking about its various elements, you can make sure that from the start you are all on the same page.
- Send your client a mood board that reflects the direction you want to take the project in so that they can really grasp your idea – the best way to present your ideas is visually.
- Your client may have a different idea in their head but a really talented designer listens to their client's wants and needs and transforms them into what they see as the best and most appealing outcome. If, after a thorough discussion with the client, you find that their expectations and wants are far from what you would like to deliver, if you're in a position to turn down that job, it may be worth politely letting them know that another designer may be better suited to help them. There's nothing wrong with doing this.
- Make sure there is an approval process in place so the client is aware of how many changes they are allowed within their budget.
- Send through your designs with a detailed description so that the client understands the reasoning behind the design. Often people don't realise why you have chosen certain colours, for example.

- Cover yourself financially. Require a payment to commence the project and a final payment before you deliver the product.

Following these tips will really help to streamline your relationship with a client. I have found that when you deliver your work, the client will often be thrilled, as they couldn't have imagined what you would come up with or how you would interpret their brief.

How to keep clients returning time after time

DO:

- Keep a wealth of ideas coming when there is a design challenge.
- Have something that makes you different to other designers (my special skills are illustration and watercolour).
- Be polite and courteous when discussing differences in opinion, and make sure you can back up your arguments.
- Always be on time for meetings.
- Deliver the project on or before deadline.

DON'T:

- Be slapdash, or have a 'that'll do' attitude.
- Copy other people's work. You can be influenced but do not plagiarise.
- Say, 'Sorry, I forgot' (the client needs to feel that they are the most important person to you).
- Yell or become argumentative when they want to make a change or are unsure about your design.
- Say, 'I don't know'. If you can't think of a solution immediately, let them know that you will do some research and get back to them.
- Shut them down when they are explaining what they want (listening is key).
- Not deliver and then go AWOL. (Yes, people do this!)

Marketing through social media

Social media is such an important tool for us creatives as it's a visually vibrant space. Capitalise on it by doing these things:

- Try to predominantly showcase your own work. I know it's great to showcase others' work from time to time to show that you have been influenced by and/or support them, but a client usually wants to receive the kind of work that they see on your socials. So make that work yours.
- On platforms such as Instagram or Facebook, make your feed visually appealing by following a colour scheme or a pattern. This can demonstrate that you have a beautiful eye for pairing images.
- People want to be happy when they come to your space, so make it that way through the visuals and messages you are projecting.
- Be positive, support other creatives and never vent (seriously, it's the biggest turn-off and the fastest way to make yourself look unprofessional and develop unneeded enemies).

Adapting your skills and services over time

Although the foundations of design remain largely the same over time, there are so many different tools we can use and so many areas and industries in which we can now use our skills.

Try to keep up with new technology and new platforms so that you don't get left behind.

Stay curious and adaptable.

Bec here, jumping in to say: Can confirm.

When I was the only one running The Comms Department eight years ago, I mostly offered traditional publicity services.

But the media industry is changing so much that I knew I'd need to quickly adapt if I wanted to secure great clients and be able to make a decent income.

So we now offer a variety of services, from managing social media accounts and media training to corporate and internal comms and crisis management.

The danger with adapting too much is that you can stray too far from what you're really great at, and then you don't deliver an amazing result.

So we countered this by setting up four or five services (that require a very similar skill set that we all have), which we then chose to apply to a select group of industries – media, entertainment, travel and lifestyle.

When the economic impact from the 2020 coronavirus pandemic hit, this diversification of services and industries – combined with being nimble and adaptable – not only saved our company, it actually allowed us to thrive.

Because we hadn't put all our eggs in one basket, when our clients in heavily affected industries had to put their work with us on hold, we still had other clients to carry us through. We also quickly identified the most-needed services during this fast-moving time – particularly in crisis management, internal and corporate comms, social media messaging, and comms training – and secured more of that work.

And because our team had already been working remotely for eight years, when much of the world's workforce was suddenly having to adjust to working from home for the first time, we positioned ourselves as the leading experts in this area. To help everyone, we provided all our tips and tricks for successfully working from home, and we spread the word via media stories, podcast interviews, social media posts and webinars. Because this expertise was highly valued and sought after, it resulted in more exposure for The Comms Department, which in turn led to us securing more clients.

> **So know what you're good at, look at how you can adapt your skills or learn new ones to fit the changing needs of clients, and then work hard to service that niche.**

CHAPTER 16

BOOKS I LOVE

to help shape the way you work, live, lead and love

you've
got
this

Who loves a great reading recommendation? I know I do.

The knowledge gained from books – whether physical books, ebooks, or audiobooks – can help to shape the way that we work, live, lead and love.

> Books open our eyes to worlds beyond our own and offer creative inspiration.
>
> By simply reading or listening to books, we also start to discover how an engaging story is created. And it's important for anyone who wants to remain in business in this changing world to develop this communication skill.
>
> Tech can do a lot already and machines' capabilities will only increase in the years ahead. But machines will likely never have the ability we humans do to craft a creative and compelling story that can rapidly pivot and adapt to an audience's nuanced responses. Nor can bots conjure unique and exciting ideas. Both of these things will give you a competitive edge no matter how times change.

So, these are just some of the books that have had a positive impact on me. I hope that you enjoy them too (I'd also love to hear your recommendations – please Tweet them to me at @becbrowncomms).

Business books

The E-Myth Revisited: Why most small businesses don't work and what to do about it by Michael E. Gerber. This book has been around for a long time and has had several revisions to keep it current. And that's because it's a gem. If you're thinking of starting a business, I suggest you read it first. I did, and I put a lot of its advice into action, and it worked.

Gretchen Rubin is a best-selling author who digs deep into human nature. *The Four Tendencies: The indispensable personality profiles that reveal how to make your life better (and other people's lives better, too)* explains her theory that we all fit into four 'tendencies': Upholders, Questioners, Obligers, and Rebels. Because our tendency shapes our behaviour, understanding which one we have, and which ones others in our lives have, can make all our lives easier.

Jonathan Raymond's *Good Authority: How to become the leader your team is waiting for* is the book I wish I read long before I became a manager or a boss. I regularly re-read it now to remind myself how I should be leading, and why it's best to do it in the way he suggests.

Think One Team: The revolutionary 90-day plan that engages employees, connects silos and transforms organisations by **Graham Winter** is a book I picked up in an airport newsagency while waiting for a delayed flight. I won't lie, it caught my eye because it had meerkats on the cover. Clever marketing strategy on their part! After I skimmed through it I realised how much insight it had to offer. This is the perfect book to teach you how to create a team that works beautifully together, for the benefit of each other and your company.

Someone I'll always have a crush on is **Jamila Rizvi**. And her book ***Not Just Lucky: Why women do the work but don't take the credit*** will give you the insight you need to start fighting not only for your own success, but also for a more inclusive and equal workplace that we can all enjoy together. This book is a confidence builder, a knowledge giver, and a call to arms. It combines case studies, research and Jamila's own experience in politics and media. And without realising that you could, after reading it you'll love and respect Jamila even more.

Pioneering psychologist **Angela Duckworth's *Grit: The power of passion and perseverance*** was an eye-opener when I first read it. It's about what goes through your head when you fail, and how that – not talent or luck – makes all the difference to your ongoing success. Angela's teachings have made me agile when I've felt I've hit a roadblock and have picked me up and dusted me off when I've felt like a failure. The podcast interviews she's done are also well worth a listen.

Finance books

If your income is low and your debts high, try to educate yourself so you're not living from pay cheque to pay cheque or feeling stressed about your financial future. For the price of a few coffees or a lipstick, learning how to manage your finances is 100 per cent worth it. And when the moment comes when you start earning a great income, it's incredibly exciting. But it's another thing entirely to know how to manage that income, so you'll want to be equipped. You've worked hard to be where you are, so make sure you set yourself up to enjoy the rewards. And with the help of these easy to read books, it's simpler than you would think.

The Barefoot Investor: The only money guide you'll ever need by **Scott Pape** has become one of the best-selling Australian books ever. It's successful because it's simple and funny, and it's genuinely changed people's finances for the better time and time again. I love how Scott gives you easy and practical 'do this, then do that' advice, and how he knows that if it's too complicated, you'll never do it.

Unf*ck Your Finances by **Melissa Browne** is 'the essential guide to becoming financially adult'. Like *Barefoot,* it offers clear, easy-to-follow advice and teaches you how to set yourself up to save – and you get to throw the traditional definition of budgeting out the door. I'm a sucker for a swear word, so that also helps.

Effie Zahos was the editor of *Money* magazine and is savvy and smart. There's not a lot she doesn't know about personal finances, which is why I'd give her book ***A Real Girl's Guide To Money: From Converse to Louboutins*** a go.

Life books (which can help with life, love AND your career)

Brené Brown is a research professor who's spent more than twenty years studying courage, vulnerability, shame and empathy. She has written five number-one *New York Times* bestsellers and you may have seen her Netflix special. Two of her books are standouts to me: ***Daring Greatly: How the courage to be vulnerable transforms the way we live, love, parent, and lead*** and ***Dare to Lead: Brave work. Tough conversations. Whole hearts***, a book that also belongs in my favourite business books section. To sum up Brené's ethos: you need to walk through vulnerability to get to courage. And this usually means doing something that I often mutter to myself when I'm feeling uncomfortable: 'embrace the suck'. Yep, there are things that suck, or that you suck at, but the only way past it is through it. She shows you how.

I've already talked a lot about **Ryan Holiday's** writing, and I highly recommend that you give his books a go. He uses real-life examples from history, which make his points easy to undertand and very memorable. Two of his books present concepts I now try to follow as they make my life a lot easier and happier: ***Ego Is the Enemy: The fight to master our greatest opponent,*** a terrific read about how your ego gets in your way, what you can do about it and why you'll want to; and ***The Obstacle Is the Way: The ancient art of turning adversity to***

advantage, which presents another way of looking at the 'when one door closes, another door opens' idea.

We met neuroscientist Dr Kerry Spackman in chapter ten, 'Overcoming setbacks & dealing with change'. His book ***The Winner's Bible: Rewire your brain for permanent change*** is one I recommend if you're looking for a deeper understanding of the best way to work towards certain goals and how to make your brain work for you, not against you. I like his values too – he encourages his readers to be well-rounded people who are also nice human beings so his advice steers you towards a lovely balance of financial and lifestyle success.

In Western culture, a lot of power has been given to those who are extroverted. Susan Cain's *Quiet: The power of introverts in a world that can't stop talking* helps to explain why there's power and beauty in introversion too.

Spencer Johnson's *Peaks and Valleys: Making good and bad times work for you – at work and in life* is an easy, quick read, and if you ever feel as if you're on a roller-coaster and want some stability in your life, this book will get you thinking about how to achieve that. It's also cleverly written as fiction, which makes the examples very relatable and memorable.

Eckhart Tolle has written so many thought-provoking books, but two of them – ***A New Earth: Awakening to your life's purpose*** and ***The Power of Now: A guide to spiritual enlightenment*** – have really helped me to learn how to be more present, to ditch my anxious mindset, and to stop listening to the unhelpful thoughts that pop into my head. They have also helped me to learn how to grow my business and to keep my edge while also being content with what I already have. For me, that's the ultimate goal.

Many of these book recommendations have been about the mind; well, this one's for your physical body. Dr Kelly McGonigal has written *The Joy of Movement: How exercise helps us find happiness, hope, connection, and courage* with her trademark blend of science and storytelling. We all know that exercise is good for our health, but many of us find it a real chore. Drawing on neuroscience, philosophy, biology, anthropology, anecdotes and more, instead of focusing on *why* you should move more, she explains *how* to fall in love with movement, which is intertwined with some of the most basic human joys and is a powerful antidote to depression, anxiety, and loneliness. This book's been a real motivator to me when I'm in two minds about stepping away from the computer or getting off the couch. I recall key takeaways that put a smile on my face and make me put my sneakers on and head out the door.

I talked briefly earlier about my struggles with eating disorders. In my tweens and for almost twenty years, on and off, I battled a trifecta of anorexia, bulimia and binge eating. If you or someone you love is struggling, please know that reaching out for help is one of the best things you'll ever do. And because everyone is different, you will need to look at tools and therapy that will work best for you.

For me, recovery was a combination of things. One was regular visits to an experienced clinical psychologist who specialised in eating disorders. We used a combination of therapies including CBT (cognitive behavioural therapy), journaling, mindfulness and meditation. In Australia, you can go to a GP to obtain a mental health treatment plan to receive subsidised psychologist appointments, which really helps with costs (something I certainly needed in my early twenties).

Later, discovering the intuitive eating methodology taught by **Marc David** from **The Institute for the Psychology of Eating** in the U.S. helped me to take another big leap forward. I read his books ***The Slow Down Diet: Eating for pleasure, energy, and weight loss*** and ***Nourishing Wisdom: A mind-body approach to nutrition and well-being***, completed his eight-week online course, and worked with one of his accredited coaches here in Australia, **Joannie Lemay** from **In Bloom**.

Award-winning registered dietitian and author **Evelyn Tribole** also offers advice on intuitive eating in ***The Intuitive Eating Workbook: Ten principles for nourishing a healthy relationship with food***, and while I haven't worked with her directly, I've heard excellent stories of success from those who have. I also found **Kathryn Hansen's** very practical book ***The Brain over Binge Recovery Guide: A simple and personalized plan for ending bulimia and binge eating disorder*** really helpful, as well as her free *Brain over Binge* podcast.

Find out more at www.inbloomproject.com, www.psychologyofeating.com, www.evelyntribole.com and www.brainoverbinge.com.

Autobiographies

My bookcase is full of autobiographies. There's something about getting inside someone else's head (and life) that's so appealing. Learning about their experiences always opens my world and seems to help me be a more empathetic, tolerant person. Getting to know others' innermost thoughts also helps me to feel less alone.

It was hard to choose my seven favourites, but here they are. Wonderfully written, by people who are genuinely excellent humans, and whose words will educate, entertain, inspire and encourage.

- *Bossypants* – Tina Fey
- *Natural Born Keller: My life and other palaver* – Amanda Keller
- *One Hundred Years of Dirt* – Rick Morton
- *The Happiest Refugee: A memoir* – Anh Do
- *The Girl with Seven Names: Escape from North Korea* – Hyeonseo Lee
- *The Ride of a Lifetime: Lessons in creative leadership* – Robert Iger
- *Year of Yes: How to dance it out, stand in the sun and be your own person* – Shonda Rhimes

If for some reason you find yourself too busy to get through as many books as you wish you could, you may want to consider using the **Blinkist** app – it's all about helping time-poor people read hundreds of books.

Blinkist gives you access to over 3000 bestselling non-fiction books, transformed into potent little packs you can listen to or read in just fifteen minutes.

Basically, they summarise and distil the books' content, which is great if you're looking for an overview – though not so great if you're looking for facts and information that lead to real growth and learning.

But I love the app because it helps you to work out if you really want to spend your hard-earned money on a particular book right now. One quick listen or read and you'll have a much better idea.

YOU'VE GOT THIS

I'd like to end on a story that may be familiar to you.

It's to do with **time**.

Throughout my career, especially as I was considering moving into new roles or starting my current business, I'd look around at others in the industry who were already doing it, and I'd compare myself to them.

My mind would go into overdrive.

Some thoughts were negative and paralysing, about how I wasn't as good as them.

Some thoughts were positive and spurring, about how I could do better.

But what always came up was 'but isn't it all too late?'

Leaving my music career to start in PR meant going back to uni and not holding my first official PR role until I was twenty-seven. Compared to those who had started their careers at twenty, I felt so behind.

But what I lacked in professional experience, I made up for in life experience.

When the time came to start my first PR job, being that little bit older and wiser meant that I was better equipped to work with all the very important stakeholders in the business – from the CEO to editors, to executive producers, to the international artist's manager, to the artist themselves. When I was given a team to manage, I was much better at it because of this life experience – I knew more about budgets, planning and different personality types and knew how to look at the bigger picture. And this kind of learning often only comes from navigating the real world.

All of this fast-tracked me for promotion and helped enormously when it came time to set up my own company at thirty-three. By then I had a better idea of how to manage my time and knew what kind of clients and colleagues I wanted to surround myself with; that I wanted work hours that allowed me to be at home more and actually see my husband; and that I wanted the flexibility to do all the other things I love, such as exercising, travelling and spending time with my family.

So I want to tell you that it's never too late.

> Right now you are exactly where you're supposed to be.
>
> And there's no better time than now to move forward with your goals.

One last reminder too – make sure that your goals line up with the values you outlined in chapter two. Check your notebook.

Because learning is one of my current values, my next step is to return to studying. I'm planning to do a part-time graduate diploma in organisational psychology online while I continue to work full time at The Comms Department. At the moment I help big brands and corporations to better communicate with their staff, internally, and with their customers, externally. But in the future I want to help clients to do this at the next level, which means better understanding people and the way their brains work, and how we as humans can work together to achieve incredible things. This also ties in with my other value of compassionate connection. The diploma will probably take me three or four years, but that's nothing in the scheme of things.

I'll also continue to upskill my financial knowledge in order to be an even better CFO both at work and at home, so I plan to keep taking courses across accounting and commercial strategy.

Because the time will pass anyway, and I may as well do something with that time.

If I'm lucky enough to be alive on this earth and to live in a country where we're fortunate to be able to back-pay our education, saying 'it's too late' feels like a cop-out. I feel like I owe it to the world to try to be a better person, even if this means only taking a tiny step in this direction each day.

Has 'it's too late' been an excuse of yours? What could you do right now, today, to move past that?

I also want to tell you about one other time-tool that's changed my daily life.

It's made me less stressed, anxious and apathetic.

It's made me more creative, friendly, tolerant and joyful.

And it's the simplest concept ever.

> **It's trying to live each moment in the now.**
>
> **It's being present.**

When we are entirely in the present, the angst falls away.

If we're constantly looking back on what happened yesterday, last week, last month, last year, or years ago, we aren't truly living. We're robbing ourselves.

That doesn't mean we can't learn from the past. Spending time reflecting on what has and hasn't worked in our lives, and discovering how past experiences may have shaped us, is healthy.

But settling down and living in the past in your head isn't.

Being in the present also means discarding those old stories we may tell ourselves. I used to say things such as, 'I'm not good at maths, I'm the creative one in the family so I should stick to that', 'I have problems around food thanks to having had eating disorders' and 'I'm a very anxious person.' But it was all crap. These were just stories I'd repeat so much that I made them fact. Discovering that I didn't always have to believe the thoughts that popped into my head wasn't easy – and still isn't easy. But if I can do this, with practice, anyone can.

The same goes for the future.

If you spend every moment thinking about what's ahead – tomorrow, next week, next year or beyond – you're robbing yourself of what is right in front of you.

But what does 'being in the present' mean for planning for the future and working towards goals? How do you build your empire or feel excitement about what's ahead while still remaining focused on the present?

Well, you still need to do the planning. But set time aside to do it.

And when you do it, and enjoy the dreamy anticipation of that exciting business you're going to start or that tropical holiday you're going to go on, you do it with your full attention and focus, mindfully.

An added bonus is that being in the moment gives you a mental break and helps to sharpen your mind. So when you move to that next stage of 'doing' (such as setting up your business or booking your holiday accommodation, which, while fun, can still be challenging and tiring), you'll have more energy and clarity.

If this next story resonates with you, know that you're certainly not alone. I've lost count of the number of friends and colleagues – from parents to students, employees to bosses, and entry-level graduates to high-flying executives – who have experienced this.

So here it is:

I used to think that worry and anxiety would give me an edge.

That by worrying, I'd have a list of potential situations that could arise and cause me unhappiness.

And I thought that once I knew what they were, I could take action to stop bad things from happening.

I'd worry that:

- I'd make a mistake at work and get fired
- I'd somehow offend someone and they'd start talking negatively about me to everyone
- my partner would lose interest in me and leave
- we'd lose clients and not get any more
- there wouldn't be enough money coming in to pay everyone's salaries
- my loved ones would have an accident, get sick, or die.

This constant cycle of worry took up so much time.

As did scrambling every day to try to make sure none of these awful things came true.

This was my strategy:

- Scared of getting fired? Well, just be perfect, and, if you fail at that, try to hide any mistakes.

- Scared of accidentally offending someone? Become a massive people pleaser, to the extent that you do and say things you don't mean or believe in so that people will like you.
- Scared of your partner leaving? That's easy – be the perfect trophy wife. Be extra loving, be sexy, be perfect. And if that fails, leave them first.
- Need to keep clients? Do whatever it takes. Anything. Even if they're lousy people with lousy ethics. Work ridiculous hours, go above and beyond every single minute of every day. Be better than everyone. Beat yourself up if that's not possible.
- Concerned that you won't have money to pay your team? Pay them all first and leave nothing for yourself. Check your bank account every five minutes to make sure your money is still there, and change your passwords daily.
- Nervous for your loved ones? Ring them constantly. Ask them if they locked the door and turned the stove and iron off. Check their health and travel insurance. Ask if they have been to the doctor and what the doctor said. Ask if they're staying off the phone while driving, wearing sunscreen, eating healthy food . . .

Reading this list now makes me feel sick. And exhausted. And obviously very grateful that I've moved on from this.

Because the root of all my worry was fear. I was bloody scared. And when I acted from a place of fear, the result was never pretty.

> What I needed to learn is that trying to control everything is pointless. The only thing we can really control is our thoughts. And even if thoughts continue to pop up that aren't helpful, we can still control how much attention we pay to them.
>
> Importantly, there's a big difference between mindless worrying (living in the future) and planning (consciously setting time to think about the future, from here in the present).

Worrying takes you away from now. But small amounts of dedicated planning time allow you to stay in the now.

And in my experience, it's planning – calmly, consciously, without fear as your motivator – that really gives you an edge.

> My final piece of advice is to remember that knowing you're right where you're supposed to be and being fully present are thought processes you need to cultivate daily.

You're never going to wake up and magically find that it's all easy.

Every hour of every day, you need to bring yourself back to being present and calm.

Some days it'll be simple.

Other days it'll feel like a constant battle.

But over time, like any habit, it'll become easier. And the benefits will blow your mind.

Thank you for reading this book – we truly hope it's been helpful.

> Our wish is that you get as much happiness and fulfillment from your work, and from those you work with, as we do.

You've got this – we can't wait to see you shine.

Bec & Inga x

If you'd like to get in touch with either of us – if you have questions or feedback – please head to our socials or email us at **hello@thecommsdepartment.com.au**. We'd love to meet you.

- becbrowncommunications
- becbrowncomms
- becbrowncommunications
- thecommsdepartment
- thecommsdeptHQ
- thecommsdepartment
- thecommsdepartment.com.au
- inkling_design
- inklingdesign.com.au

GIVING BACK

We all need a helping hand from time to time. It's what makes us human. I know that I've benefited greatly from the compassion and generosity of others.

And if you've been fortunate enough to receive things such as a great public school education, a university degree you can back-pay, or the luxury of choosing your own career path, I believe it's your duty to help others who may not have been so lucky in whatever way you can – big or small. It's as simple as that.

Inga and I are incredibly lucky to have had these opportunities. Not everyone has such a strong start in life.

But everyone deserves to fulfil their potential in a way that truly makes them happy.

> A portion of the proceeds from every copy of *You've Got This* sold will be going to two brilliant charities to help even more women live their most successful lives.
>
> By purchasing this book, you're helping to making a difference – thank you very much for your support.

- **The Life Changing Experiences Foundation** helps Australia's most marginalised girls grow into strong independent women capable of taking their place in the world.

  The Foundation successfully delivers two programs: No Limits 4 Girls and SISTER2sister.

  No Limits 4 Girls (NL4G) is a wellbeing workshop series delivered to year 7 students, designed to empower young women by increasing their resilience, emotional intelligence and stress management skills, creating a strong foundation for personal growth. NL4G has been designed as a referral pathway for the SISTER2sister program, which supports girls from year 7 to year 12.

The SISTER2sister mentoring program is an evidence-based and trauma-informed youth development program that provides structured mentoring, education, welfare support and crisis intervention services to vulnerable or disadvantaged teenage girls (Little Sisters) aged 12–18 years old.

By equipping the Little Sisters with crucial survival and life skills, the resilience to overcome challenges, and a safe environment fostering self-worth, the SISTER2sister mentoring program empowers these girls to break the cycle of abuse and neglect and to make positive choices that help them turn their lives around.

As a result of these programs, hundreds of young women have completed their education and taken up further study or workplace opportunities that would otherwise have been out of their reach.

www.lifechangingexperiences.org

- **Fitted for Work** is the first Australian organisation of its kind, dedicated to helping women experiencing disadvantage to get work and keep it.

  They do this through a suite of tailored pre- and post-employment programs and services that are available nationally, that develop women's confidence, self-esteem, skills and knowledge.

  Fitted for Work's vision is economic independence and empowerment for women. They see a future where women contribute equally to the positive transformation of society through their role in the workplace. They know that when women have hope, dignity, confidence and economic security through work, the flow-on effect is transformational, to them, to their families and to society as a whole. They welcome all women, including cisgender, transgender, non-binary and gender non-conforming people and all those who identify as women, who have experienced disadvantage and are seeking employment.

  Fitted for Work believe that when a woman is fitted for work, she is fitted for life.

  www.fittedforwork.org

THANKS

This book has been a labour of love that began ten years ago with a blog, which turned into this book's first draft. But it really developed over the past two years as more and more smart, creative graduates and professionals came to me for career advice. And this book needed to take this long to create because, although I didn't realise it at the time, I needed the business and life lessons I gained over that period to write what I have. I've spent recent months editing and revising the content to make sure every little piece of advice is 100 per cent current and relevant in these fast-moving times.

While I can't fit all the people who have helped to shape my career and my life on these pages, if we've ever crossed paths, know that you've had an effect on me and, in turn, this book. So thank you.

Those who need to be namechecked with heartfelt thanks include my wonderful mum Yvonne and dad Ian, my brother Andrew and sisters Jodie and Sarah, their beautiful partners Nicki, Michael and Jason, all my nieces and nephews and their partners and children, and my incredible in-laws Kevin, Mary, Tash, Ray and Luca, for the inspiration, love, care and support they give and for their understanding of the hours that I put in.

Thank you to the brilliant The Comms Department team, past and present, many of whom are both colleagues and friends – especially Tina Liptai, Shaheeda Chelat, Yanna Moutzouris, Michael Hickson, Lauren Bradley, Sacha Monk and Kylee Pryor.

To my media friends, those clever and curious journalists, producers, writers and content makers who seek every day to inform, entertain and influence – I so admire you. You make my working life fun and interesting and you keep my skills sharp! To those of you who began as a media contact and have gone on to become a very dear friend – you know who you are – thank you. A particularly big thankyou to Amanda Keller, Leigh Campbell, Shelly Horton, Ash London, Sarah Stinson, Sally Obermeder, Kylie Gillies, Baz DuBois, Jackie O, Yumi Stynes, Angela Bishop, Sarah Harris, Richard Wilkins, Brendan Jones, Nic McClure, JMo, Briana Domjen, Ben Fordham, Rachel Lees and Deb Clay, who each inspire me daily in different ways and who have been incredibly supportive of my career over many years.

Thanks to my industry friends – PRs, marketers, managers, musicians, business owners and more, who get up every day and give it their all, while remaining kind, brave and adventurous, and with a cracking sense of humour – especially Anthony Xydis, Lauren Miller, Tim Ross, Joey and Rich Toutounji, Jasmine Cruickshank, Mia Lindqvist, Joannie Lemay, Amber Lawrence, Julia Vargiu, Nadya Balzarolo, LV and Bruno Bouchet, Sean

Warner, Darren Aboud, Jason Fielding, Nick Fordham, Marina Paul, Jane Negline, Angela Ceberano, Elle Halliwell, Claire Kingston, and Simon Pryce and Lauren Hannaford (long live our ongoing 'ideas' sessions). A special shout-out too to my friends outside the industry who provide constant perspective and a much-needed break from the 24/7 media bubble, especially Fiona, Nathan, Jacqui, Moose, MOL, Libby, Jess, Bligh, Lily, Darren, Myfi, Prue, Tom, Sam and Adam.

Thank you to our TCD clients over the past eight years who allow us daily to 'do brilliant work with brilliant people', with a special nod to the entire team at Australian Radio Network, including Ciaran Davis, Duncan Campbell, Donna Gordon, Gab Cook, Steph Wolff and the rest of the marketing #DreamTeam, and the presenters, newsreaders, producers, activations and sales managers and more at the KIIS FM and Pure Gold networks, The Edge, iHeartRadio and the iHeartPodcast Network. Thanks also to the teams at Universal Music, EMI, Sony Music and Live Nation, to Tanya Deans, Natalie Chalmers and the team at Bras N Things, to Ashleigh Grier and the team at NBCUniversal's hayu, to Glenn Broadhurst, Cherie Herrmann and the team at Cover-More Travel Insurance, to Anthony Field, Murray Cook and Paul Field at The Wiggles, to Katarina Kroslakova at Primary Ideas and to Keren Ludski and the team at Red Nose. And to my past bosses who have mentored me in more ways than they realise.

Thank you to Nicky Lobo for her valuable first read-through and feedback, to Yasmin Naghavi at Media Arts Lawyers, to Kirstin Corcoran for being an open-hearted connector, and to Vanessa McCarthy at Tone Studio for being a momentum maker and bringing my vision for the design of this book to life. A huge thankyou to Penguin Random House – to Izzy Yates who, in addition to being an extraordinarily talented and dedicated commissioning editor, believed in and championed this book and its aim of having a positive effect on women's lives, all from day one. Izzy, your professionalism, enthusiasm and kindness have made this process a dream. To Mel Lane for her editing prowess (and teaching me so much in the process) and Catherine Dunk for her proofing ATD. To James Rendall for being such a clever and patient designer, audio expert Radhiah Chowdhury, marketing and publicity pros Alysha Farry, Emily Hindle and Alyssia El Gawly, sales guns Gavin Schwarcz, Belinda Conners, Janine Brown and Kaye Wright, and to Ben Fairclough and Bonny Maddah. And thank you to Justin Ractliffe and Julie Burland for saying YES.

And of course, thank you to Inga Campbell, whose beautiful illustrations are matched by her sincerity, professionalism and wonderful lead-by-example lessons in life priorities.

And finally to Dom, for being everything he is and for always believing in me.

Bec

PENGUIN BOOKS

UK | USA | Canada | Ireland | Australia

India | New Zealand | South Africa | China

Penguin Books is part of the Penguin Random House group of companies whose addresses can be found at global.penguinrandomhouse.com

Penguin Random House Australia

First published by Penguin Books in 2020

Cover and internal illustrations by Inga Campbell

Cover design by James Rendall © Penguin Random House Australia Pty Ltd

Design concept by Vanessa McCarthy and Bec Brown

Typeset in Fira Sans by James Rendall, Penguin Random House Australia

Printed and bound in China by RR Donnelley

NATIONAL LIBRARY OF AUSTRALIA

A catalogue record for this book is available from the National Library of Australia

ISBN 978 1 76089 785 7

penguin.com.au